HOW TO PLAY WINNING POKER

HOW TO PLAY
WINNING
POKER

AVERY CARDOZA

CARDOZA PUBLISHING

Visit our web site! www.cardozapub.com

Cardoza Publishing is the foremost gaming and gambling publisher in the world with a library of almost 100 up-to-date and
easy-to-read books and strategies. These authoritative works are
written by the top experts in their fields and with more than
5,000,000 books in print, represent the best-selling and most popular gaming books anywhere.

PRINTING HISTORY

First Printing	March 1987
Second Printing	November 1988
Third Printing	January 1990
Second Edition	
First Printing	April 1993
Second Printing	March 1995
Third Edition	
First Printing	January 1999

Library of Congress Catalog Card No:96-71758
ISBN:0-940685-75-2

ABOUT THE AUTHOR

Avery Cardoza is the foremost gambling authority in the world and best-selling author of twenty-one gambling books and advanced strategies, including *How to Win at Gambling, Secrets of Winning Slots*, and the classic, *Winning Casino Blackjack for the Non-Counter*.

Cardoza began his gambling career underage in Las Vegas as a professional blackjack player beating the casinos at their own game and was soon barred from one casino after another. In 1981, when even the biggest casinos refused him play, Cardoza founded Cardoza Publishing, which has sold more than five million books and published close to 100 gaming titles.

Though originally from Brooklyn, New York, where he is occasionally found, Cardoza has used his winnings to pursue a lifestyle of extensive traveling in exotic locales around the world.

In 1994, he established Cardoza Entertainment, a multimedia development and publishing house, to produce interactive gambling simulations that give players a taste of a real casino with animated and responsive dealers, and the full scale of bets at the correct odds. The result, *Avery Cardoza's Casino*, featuring 65 gambling variations, became an instant entertainment hit making its way onto USA Today's best-seller's list. It also catapulted Cardoza Entertainment, measured by average sales per title, as the number two seller of games in the entire industry for the first six months of 1997, ahead of such giants as Dreamworks, Microsoft, and others. Their second title, *Avery Cardoza's 100 Slots*, was a simulated slots palace with 101 machines, and became another best-seller.

Cardoza Entertainment's activities in developing an online casino for real money has attracted worldwide interest in the online gambling community. As the highest profile player in casino simulations, and the only publisher featuring actual simulations with true odds and interactive animated dealers, Cardoza Entertainment is acknowledged as the leading player in the online casino market.

To Tenzing Kernan

TABLE OF CONTENTS

10. PERCEPTIONS AND PLAYERS   111

11. BLUFFING   123

I. INTRODUCTION

Poker is the greatest and most exciting gambling game, an American tradition where rich and poor, and men and women of all classes gather around a table and vie for stakes ranging from mere pennies to thousands of dollars. No other game provides the challenges of skill, luck and psychology, and the drama of the bluff in such a fascinating wave.

In this book, we'll show you how to conquer these challenges and be a winner at poker!

We cover the major poker variations – draw poker: jacks or better and anything opens, seven card high stud, high-low stud, hold'em, Omaha high-low 8 or better, lowball: draw poker and seven card low stud (Razz) – and show the basics of play for each of these games. We discuss the differences between casino and private games and go into all the fundamentals of poker: the jargon, the rules of the games, the player's options, the ranks of hands for high, low, and wild card poker, how to bet, how to play, and everything else needed to make you an informed player.

In addition to the basic of play at each of the games, there are chapters on winning concepts, bluffing, and general strategies. You'll learn how to recognize lock, strong, marginal, and weak hands, and how to play these cards; how to play position at the table; how to use pot odds to determine the soundness of a bet; how to read opponent's playing styles and cash in on that information; how to play against opponents who bluff a lot or rarely bluff or are loose or tight players, and much, much more, so that by adjusting your play accordingly, you'll have a big edge on your opponents.

It's all here in this book. Now let's go out there and win!

2. HISTORY

Poker is as American as apple pie, a truly great gambling game whose popularity seems to grow with time. It flourishes in private homes and clubs throughout the United States and Canada, and has devotees around the world as well. For many players, the Friday night poker game has been an uninterrupted ritual for years.

The first seeds of poker drifted across the oceans from the European and Asian continents and found cultivation around the burgeoning Mississippi River port of New Orleans in the early 1800's. The Louisiana Purchase of 1803 opened up this wild and new frontier, and soon thereafter, poker began to capture the gambling spirits and imagination of the new settlers.

The original American poker game used only a 20 card deck of four suits: spades, diamonds, clubs and hearts. The deck contained four each of aces, kings, queens, jacks and 10s, one ordinal per suit. This early form did not yet recognize straights and flushes. Card games from Persia (As Nas or As), France (Poque) and Germany (Pochen or Poch) are credited with being the forerunners of poker.

By the 1840's, the full 52 card deck had been adopted, with the four suits now represented in card values of aces (high) through deuces (low). Straights and flushes made their way into the game by the late 1850's, establishing poker in its more or less modern day form.

3. THE BASICS OF POKER

OBJECT OF THE GAME

The player's object in poker is to win the money in the **pot**, the accumulation of bets and antes gathered in the center of the table. This can be done two ways. The first way is to have the highest ranking hand at the **showdown**, the final act in poker, where all active player's hands are revealed to see who's got the best. The second way is when all other players drop out of play. In these instances, there is no showdown and the remaining player automatically wins the pot.

PARTICIPANTS

Poker can be played with two players to as many as the 52 card deck can support, usually around eight or nine players. One version of poker, hold 'em, can theoretically support as many as 20 players, though more than 11 players is rarely seen in any poker variation.

In a private game, one of the players is designated as the **dealer**, the person who shuffles and deals the cards to the players. The deal changes with each hand, rotating around the table in a clockwise direction, with each player having a chance to deal. The dealer is still an active player in a private game and enjoys no advantage other than any positional edge he may have for the particular game played.

In casino poker, the dealer is a house employee and non-player. In addition to shuffling and dealing the cards, the house dealer is responsible for the supervision and general running of the game, making sure that all betting is in order and that the proper procedures of play are followed.

In poker variations where the dealer enjoys a positional advantage, such as hold'em, lowball, Omaha, and draw poker, a **button** is utilized to designate the imaginary dealer's position. The button rotates around the table, one spot at a time, in clockwise fashion, so that like the private game, each player in turn has a chance to enjoy the advantages of acting last.

Each player in poker plays by himself and for himself alone against all other players. Collusion or partnership play are illegal and are considered cheating.

THE DECK OF CARDS

Poker is played with a standard 52 card deck containing four suits of thirteen cards each: clubs, diamonds, spades and hearts. The cards are valued in descending order with the ace being the most powerful and followed respectively by the king, queen, jack, ten, nine, eight, seven, six, five, four, three and, finally, the **deuce** or two, that being the lowest ranked card.

The Four Suits

The king, queen and the jack are known as **picture cards** or **face cards**.

The four suits in poker have no basic value in the determination of winning hands, and, as we shall see, it is not the value of the individual cards that reign supreme in poker, but the *combination of cards* which determine the value of a player's hand.

CARD ABBREVIATIONS

We will refer to the cards by the following commonly used symbols: ace (A), king (K), queen (Q), jack (J), and all others directly by their numerical value. Thus, the three will be indicated by (3), nine by (9) and the ten by (10).

RANK OF HANDS: HIGH POKER

Poker is generally played as high poker, and listed here are the relative rankings of hands in descending order, from best to worst. Later, in the lowball: draw poker section, we'll discuss that poker variation and the ranking of low poker hands.

Note that all poker hands eventually consist of five cards, regardless of the variation played.

ROYAL FLUSH

An A, K, Q, J, and 10, all of the same suit is called a **royal flush**. For example, the A♠, K♠, Q♠, J♠, and 10♠, all in spades, is a royal flush. The odds of being dealt a royal flush in a five card poker game is one in 649,740.

The royal flush is the most powerful hand in poker and one a player may never see in a lifetime of play. In the unlikely event that two players hold a royal flush, the hand is a tie and the pot split.

Royal Flush

STRAIGHT FLUSH

Five cards of the same suit in numerical sequence, such as the Q♦, J♦, 10♦, 9♦, and 8♦, is called a **straight flush**. This particular example is called a queen high straight flush since the queen is the highest ranking card. The straight flush is the second most powerful hand in poker.

Straight Flush

When two straight flushes are in competition for the pot, the straight flush with the highest ranking card wins. Thus, a queen high straight flush beats out a 10 high straight flush. If two players hold equivalently ranked straight flushes, such as 9♣, 8♣, 7♣, 6♣, and 5♣, and

9♥, 8♥, 7♥, 6♥, and 5♥, then the hand is a tie and the pot is split. Suits have no predominance over one another in poker.

The ace must be used as either the highest card in the straight flush (an ace high hand being a royal flush) or the lowest card, as in A♦, 2♦, 3♦, 4♦, and 5♦, to be valid. The hand of Q♣, K♣, A♣, 2♣, and 3♣ is not a straight flush, simply a flush only.

FOUR OF A KIND

Four cards of identical rank, such as the hand J, J, J, J, 3, is called **a four of a kind**, and is almost a sure win in straight poker (poker without a wild card). The odd card in the above example, the 3, is irrelevant and has no bearing on the rank of the hand.

When two players hold a four of a kind, the higher ranking four of a kind will win the hand. For example, J, J, J, J, 3 beats out 7, 7, 7, 7, A.

Four-of-a-Kind

FULL HOUSE

A **full house** consists of three cards of identical rank along with two cards of an identical but different rank. 3, 3, 3, A, A and 5,5,5,7,7 are two examples of a full house.

Full House

When two players hold full houses, it is the hand holding the higher ranking three of a kind that wins the pot. In the above example, the latter hand, 55577 is the higher ranking full house.

FLUSH

Any five cards of the same suit constitutes a **flush** in poker. A♠, K♠, 7♠, 3♠, and 2♠ is called an ace high flush in spades and Q♥, 10♥, 7♥, 5♥, 3♥ is a queen high flush in hearts.

When two or more players hold flushes, the flush with the highest ranking card wins the pot. In the above example, the ace high flush holds the higher ranking card, the ace, and is therefore the stronger hand.

Flush

If the highest ranking cards in competing flushes are of equivalent rank, then the next highest cards decide the winner, and if they too are tied, then the next cards, and so on down to the fifth card if necessary. For example, in the two flushes, K♦, Q♦, 9♦, 7♦, 6♦, and K♥, Q♥, J♥, 5♥, 2♥, the heart flush is the stronger flush

for its third highest ranking card, the jack, is higher ranking than the 9, the diamond flush's third highest ranking
card.

When all five cards of competing flushes are identical, the hand is a tie, and the drawn winners split the
pot. Suits are of no relevance in determining a higher
ranking flush.

STRAIGHT

Five non-suited cards in sequential order, such as 10,
9, 8, 7, 6, are called a **straight**. When straights contain
an ace, the ace must serve as either the highest card in
the run, such as the ace high straight A, K, Q, J, 10, or
the lowest card, as in the five high straight, 5, 4, 3, 2, A.
The cards Q, K, A, 2, 3, is not a straight and is merely an
ace high hand. It is beaten by even a lowly pair.

Straight

When two or more straights are in competition, the
straight with the highest ranking card takes the pot. A 9
high straight beats out a 7 high straight. When two
straights are of equal value, the hand is a tie and the pot
is split.

THREE OF A KIND

Three matched cards of identical value along with
two odd cards (unmatched) are called a **three of a kind**.
777Q2 is called "three sevens" or "trip sevens."

When two players hold a three of a kind, the player with the higher ranking triplets takes the pot. Three jacks, JJJ 34, beats out the trip eight hand of 888 Q5.

Three-of-a-Kind

TWO PAIR

Two sets of equivalently valued or "paired" cards along with an unmatched card, are called two pairs. 10 10 88 5 is a two paired hand and is called "tens up" or "tens over eights," since the tens are the higher ranking pair. Similarly, AA 33 J is called "aces up" or "aces over threes."

Two Pair

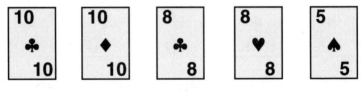

If more than one player holds a two pair hand, the winner would be the player holding the higher ranked of the two paired hand. JJ 77 K beats out 10 10 99 A. When the higher ranking pairs are identical, the next paired cards determine the winner. 88 44 10 loses to 88 55 9. When both pairs are evenly matched, the higher ranking fifth card, the odd card, determines the victor. If all cards are equally ranked, such as 55 33 2 and 55 33 2, then the hand is a tie and the pot is split.

ONE PAIR

One set of identically valued cards along with three unmatched cards are called a pair. The hand 22 84 A is referred to as "a pair of twos." Pairs are ranked in order of value from aces, the highest, down to the deuces, the lowest. Thus, a pair of aces beats out a pair of kings, and a pair of nines wins over a pair of sixes.

One Pair

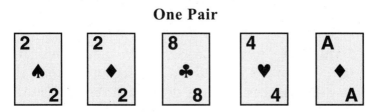

When two players hold equally paired hands, the highest odd card held decides the winner. 88 Q 73 triumphs over 88 J 97. If the highest unmatched cards are also equivalently valued, then the next highest cards are compared and then the last cards if necessary. JJ 10 98 beats out JJ 10 97. If all cards are identical, then the hand is a tie and the pot is split.

HIGH CARD

A hand containing five unmatched cards, that is, lacking any of the above combinations - a pair, two pairs, three of a kind, straights, flushes, full houses, four of a kind, straight flushes or royal flushes - is determined by its highest ranking card. The hand A 10 9 8 7 is considered an "ace high" hand and beats out the lesser "king high" hand of K Q J 4 3.

When the highest ranking cards are identical, the hand with the next highest card wins, and if they too are equivalent, then the next two highest are paired and so on to the fifth card. The hand K Q 7 5 2 beats out K Q 7 4 3. If all cards are identical, the hand is a draw and the pot is split.

King-High Hand

There are a total of 2,598,960 five-card combinations possible with a 52-card deck. The following chart illustrates the chances of being dealt each type of hand.

Probabilities of Five-Card Poker Hands		
Hand	**Number**	**Approximate Odds**
Royal Flush	4	649,740 to 1
Straight Flush	36	72,192 to 1
Four of a Kind*	624	4,164 to 1
Full House	3,744	693 to 1
Flush	5,108	508 to 1
Straight	10,200	254 to 1
Three of a Kind	54,912	46 to 1
Two Pair	123,552	20 to 1
One Pair	1,098,240	1.37 to 1
No Hand	1,302,540	1 to 1

*Though there are only 13 four of a kind combinations, this calculation takes into account the total of possibilities when the fifth card is figured in to make a five-card hand.

WILD CARDS

In some poker games, players will designate certain cards as **wild cards**, cards which can take on any value and suit at the holder's discretion - even as a duplicate of a card already held. Sometimes the "53rd" and "54th" cards of the deck, the jokers, are used, or players might designate the deuces or the one-eyed jacks as wild cards. Any card can be considered wild at the common consent of the players.

For example, if the deuces were used as wild cards, the hand 6 5 3 2 2 could be a straight by designating one deuce as a 7 and the other as a 4. At the showdown, the holder of this hand would represent a 7 high straight as his best total.

RANK OF HANDS: WILD CARD POKER

The only difference in the ranking of hands in wild card poker from high poker is that five of a kind in wild poker is the highest ranking hand. Otherwise, all other rankings from the royal flush down to the high card follow the same relative rankings.

Here are the relative rankings of hands, from highest to lowest, in wild card poker.

Ranks of Hands • Wild Card Poker

Five of a Kind
Royal Flush
Straight Flush
Four of a Kind
Full House
Flush
Straight
Three of a Kind
Two Pairs
One Pair
High Card Wins

RANK OF HANDS: LOW POKER

In low poker, the ranking of hands are the opposite to that of high poker, with the lowest hand being the most powerful. The ace is considered the lowest and therefore most powerful card, with the hand 5 4 3 2 A being the best low total possible. (See the lowball: draw poker section for further discussion of low poker rankings.)

MONEY AND CHIPS

Chips are the standard and accepted currency for casino and private poker games, though cash is sometimes used as well. Players prefer the use of chips for betting purposes as the handling of money at the tables is cumbersome and can slow a game down. Additionally, there's something impersonal and distant about chips, and it removes players from the reality of the actual money being won or lost.

In casino poker, the standard denominations of chips are $1, $5, $25, $100, and for big money games, $5000 and $1,000 chips can sometimes be found. In games with 25¢ and 50¢ antes, regular quarters and half dollars are also used. Though some casinos use their own color code, the typical color scheme of poker chips are : $1 – Silver, $5 – red, $25 – green, and $100 – black.

To receive chips in a casino game, give the dealer cash, and you'll receive the equivalent value back in chips. This exchange of cash for chips is called a **buy-in**. Dealers will only accept cash or chips, so if you have traveler's checks, credit cards or other forms of money, you need to exchange these for cash at the area marked **Casino Cashier**. Then, with cash in hand, you can buy chips at the poker table.

In private games, players generally use chips, though often, the game will be cash only. When chips are used, one player acts as the **bank** or **banker**, and converts player's cash buy-ins to an equivalent value in chips. The most common denominations of chips used in private games are one unit, five units, ten units, and twenty-five units. A unit can equal a penny, a dollar, or whatever value is agreed upon and set by the players.

One unit chips are generally white; five units – red; ten units – blue; and twenty-five units – yellow, though any equivalencies or colors may be used.

PRELIMINARIES OF PLAY

The dealer is responsible for shuffling the cards after each round of play so that the cards are mixed well and are in random order. The deck is then offered to a player, usually on the dealer's right, for the **cut**. This player initiates the cut by removing the top part of the deck and placing it to one side, face down. The dealer completes the cut by placing the former lower portion of the deck on top of the former upper section, thereby effecting the cut, and making the deck of cards whole again.

To be valid, a cut must go deeper than the top five cards of the deck and may not go further in than the last five. This helps prevent players who had inadvertently or otherwise seen the top or bottom cards from using the cut to undue advantage. The cut of any number of cards between these two extremes is valid and perfectly acceptable.

The game is ready to begin.

ANTES

An **ante**, also known as a **sweetener**, is a uniform bet placed by players into the pot before the cards are dealt. The size of the ante is prearranged by the players, or in a casino is set by the house, and is required of all players.

The ante is used in a majority of private poker games and virtually all casino games, and is a way to "sweeten the pie," and create more action in the game. The ante creates an immediate pot, which sharp players, under the right circumstances, may go after right from the start. Called **stealing the ante**, a player will bet forcefully in first round play hoping to force opposing players out of the pot, thereby winning the pot and the antes in it by the process of elimination.

THE PLAY OF THE GAME

After the dealer shuffles the cards and offers the cut, the deal is ready to begin. If the game requires an ante, the dealer may announce **ante-up**, a call for all players to place their antes into the pot. The center of the table is used as the area for the pot and that is where all antes and bets should be placed.

The dealer begins dealing to the player on his immediate left, and deals cards one at a time in a clockwise rotation, until each player has received the requisite number of cards for the variation being played. In casino games, where a rotating **button** is used to mark the dealer's position, the deal begins with the player to the left of the button and continues around in the same fashion as in the private game.

Like the dealing of the cards, play always proceeds in clockwise fashion, beginning in the first round, with either the player sitting to the immediate left of the dealer, or in some of the stud games, with either the high or low card opening play, as the case may be, and continues around the table until each player in turn has acted.

In later rounds though, the first player to act will vary depending on the variation being played. In the stud games, the strongest ranking open cards will open betting, and in the draw games, either the first active player to the left of the dealer will open betting or the last player to have raised or opened betting in the previous round will initiate play.

However, we'll cover the particulars of play under the games themselves and see how the betting works for the different variations.

THE PLAYER'S OPTIONS

Except for the times when a bet is mandatory, as is usually the case in the initial round of play, the first player to act in a betting round has three options: He can place a **bet**, money wagered and placed into the pot; he can **check** or **pass**, make no bet at all and pass play on to the next player while remaining an active player; or he can **fold** or **go out**, throw away his cards and forfeit future play during the current deal.

However, once a bet is placed, a player no longer has the option of checking his turn. To remain an active player, he must either **call the bet** or **see the bet**, place an amount of money into the pot equal to the bet; or he can **raise (call and raise),** call the bet and make an additional bet on top of the bet called. If a player doesn't want to bet, then he must fold and go out of play. Each succeeding player, in turn, is faced with the same options: calling, folding or raising.

To continue playing for the pot, a player must call the original bet and any raises that were made. Or a player may choose to fold his cards if he doesn't want to call the bets and raises that preceded him.

When play swings around again to the original bettor, he or she must call any previous raises to continue as an active player as must any subsequent players who have raises due, or he must fold. A player may also raise again if the raise limit hasn't been reached.

The number of raises permitted vary from game to game, but generally, casino games are limited to either three or five total raises in one round, except in instances where just two players remain, called **head to head** play, when unlimited raising is allowed. Most private games allow unlimited raising at all times.

However, a player may not raise his own bet. He may only raise another player's bet or raise.

Play continues until the last bet or raise is called by all active players, and no more bets or raises are due any player. The betting round is now completed and over.

One important rule of poker etiquette is that player's check, bet, raise or fold in their proper turn only. This rule must always be respected by all players.

Some games use a **blind**, a mandatory bet that is made by the first player to act in the opening round of play. This player, called the **blind bettor**, must make the blind bet regardless of the hand he or she holds. The blind is a forced bet and forces immediate action in a poker game. When there are two blinds, as is the case in many games, then the next player in turn will be forced to make a blind bet as well. Often these two bettors are know as the small blind and the big blind. The small blind, the first player to make the forced bet, is usually required to bet half the minimum bet while the full blind, is required to bet equal to the minimum. For example, in a $5-$10 game, the small blind would bet $5 and the big blind would bet $10.

Players cannot check after a blind bet is made and must either call the blind, raise or fold. Otherwise, play proceeds the same as in games which don't use a blind. The amount of a blind bet varies, but is usually less than or equal to the minimum bet.

Check and raise, a player's raising of a bet after already checking in a round, is usually not allowed in private games, though many casino games permit its use. Before sitting down to play in a game, ask if check and raise is allowed.

BETTING LIMITS (LIMIT POKER)

Betting in poker is generally structured in a two-tiered level, with the lower level of betting occurring before the draw in the draw poker variations or in the early rounds of the stud games, and the upper level occurring after the draw in the draw poker games and in the later rounds in the stud variations. Some commonly used betting structures are $1-$2, $1-$3, $5-$10, and $15-$30, though other limits are found as well.

In a $5-$10 limit game, when the lower limit of betting is in effect, all bets and raises must be in $5 increments, and when the upper range is in effect, all bets and raises must be in $10 increments.

In the discussions covering the individual poker variations, we'll discuss when the lower and upper ranges of betting are in play for each of the games.

The betting limits of casino games are generally posted above the table, or can be found out by asking the dealer or one of the players. The betting limits of private games are prearranged and agreed upon by the players before play.

TABLE STAKES

Table stakes is the rule in casino poker and almost all private games, and states that a player's bet or call of a bet may not exceed the amount of money he has on the table in front of him. For example, if the bet due a player is $25, and he only has $10 remaining on the table, this player is considered **tapped-out**, and may only call the bet to the tune of $10. He is not allowed to withdraw money from his wallet, borrow from others or receive credit during a deal. That is permissible only before the cards are dealt.

In the above example, the remaining $15 and all future monies bet during this hand would be segregated into a separate pot. The tapped-out player can still receive cards until the showdown and play for the original pot, but he can no longer take part in the betting, and has no interest in the side pot. The other players however, can continue to bet and wager against each other for the side pot as well.

Should the tapped-out player have the best hand at the showdown, he receives only the money in the original pot, before he tapped-out. The side pot is won by the player having the best hand among the remaining players. Should one of the other players hold the overall best hand, that player wins both the original and the side pot.

If only one other bettor remains when a player taps out, then there is no more betting, and cards are played out until the showdown. In the above example, the opposing player would have $15 of his $25 bet returned to him, since only $10 of his bet can be called. At the showdown, the best hand would win the existing pot.

POT LIMIT AND NO LIMIT

Poker is sometimes played as pot limit or no limit, betting structures often used in high stakes poker games. **Pot limit** games allow players to bet any amount up to the current size of the pot, but no more. For example, if the pot holds $75, the largest allowable bet is $75. If a player then bets pot limit and places $75 more into the pot, the pot would now contain $150. The betting limit is now set at a maximum of $150.

No limit poker is even a wilder version and states that a player's maximum bet is limited only by the table stakes rule. The World Series of Poker played at the Horseshoe Casino in Las Vegas every year plays no limit style of hold'em poker with a $10,000 buy-in.

Pot limit and no limit poker are too vicious for the average player (unless comfortable maximum betting ranges are set by the players) and should not be considered by anyone but top level players with big purses. In this book, we'll assume just the limit variety of poker, the game almost universally played by most players in private and casino games.

SAMPLE ROUND OF BETTING

For illustrative purposes, let's follow the play in the first betting round of a private draw poker: anything opens game. This game is played without a blind (as is jacks or better), and the first player to act may check or bet as desired. In the other games we discuss - hold'em, lowball: draw poker and the seven card stud variations - the opening player has no such luxury and must either make a mandatory opening bet or fold (when allowed). In these games, checking is not allowed in first round play.

(We'll look at the particular rules of play for each game in the individual games sections, and show which player is the first to act in a betting round and whether that player must make a mandatory opening bet.)

Let's pick up the action now and see how the betting works. The eight players have agreed to play with a $1 ante, so the pot holds $8 before any of the cards are dealt. The participants are, in order, clockwise from the dealer, Julian, Eddie-boy, Vicenzo, Fay, Donto, Flavian, Uncle J. and Big Phil (the current dealer).

They are playing **dealer's choice**, a rule which allows each successive dealer to choose the variation played during his deal. In casino poker games, dealer's choice is not played, and players are limited to playing the variations designated for their table. If a player wishes to play a different variation, he or she must switch to a table offering the game desired.

Big Phil is the current dealer and has chosen draw poker: anything opens as the game he wants to deal. The player sitting to the immediate left of the dealer goes first in draw poker, and after the cards are dealt all players await Julian's decision.

Julian raps on the table with his knuckles, a nonverbal signal used in poker to indicate that a player is checking. He may also indicate checking by saying "Check" or "Pass" or some such communication. Eddie-boy and Vicenzo, in turn, check as well, and pass play on to Fay, the next player.

Fay announces, "I'll bet $5," and throws a $5 chip into the pot. Now that a bet is placed, no player can check and remain in the game.

Donto, sitting at Fay's left, decides his hand isn't worth $5 and flips his cards face down toward the dealer. Donto is no longer a participant in the pot and forfeits his $1 ante. He must wait until the next deal to resume play.

Flavian draws a big puff out of his cigar, "Cuban," he claims, and throws $10 into the pot, calling Fay's $5 bet and raising it $5 more. He announces, "$10 to you, Uncle J."

Raises, like bets, are made by the physical placement of chips in the pot area and, as is often the custom in a private game, they may be announced as well. Raising may be indicated by saying, "I'll raise you" or "I'll call that bet and raise," or any such communication that clearly indicates that a raise is being made.

Uncle J. is either daunted by the $10 due him or the cigar, for he folds. Big Phil, the dealer for this round of play, calls the $5 bet and the $5 raise, and re-raises $5 more. He places $15 into the pot.

Flavians' cigar whirls across his mouth like a brigate cannon searching out new targets, and sends the long overdue ashes crashing against the dizzying colors of his Hawaiian short-sleeved shirt. One ash, still hot, works its way into a palm tree, and then fades away in lasting glory.

Play now returns to Julian, who had checked earlier. To play, he must call $15 worth of bets, one $5 bet plus two $5 raises. He throws his cards in without hesitation, and is followed by Eddie-boy who does the same. Vicenzo, who had also checked, bets the $15. He may not raise, for this private games disallows check and raise. However, if check and raise was permitted, he would be allowed to raise $5 more.

Since this is the first round of betting, all bets and raises are in $5 increments. $10 bets and raises are not allowed this round.

Fay plays next, and she must call the two $5 raises of her original bet to remain playing. She may have called just one raise, but with two raises facing her and Flavian's cigar bent at a mean angle, she decides her hand is not worth $10 more, and decides to fold. She's out her earlier $5 bet and $1 ante - that money belongs to the pot.

Play passes by Donto, for he had folded earlier, and proceeds to Flavian and his cigar, the first raiser. Since his raise had been upped $5 by Big Phil, he must call that re-raise to play. The cigar rotates slowly as it weighs the possibility of raising again and then pointedly stops, aimed dead ahead at the middle of Big Phil's forehead. Another second passes, drawn out by a long puff, and then Flavian flips a $5 chip into the pot, calling Big Phil's raise.

The only active players remaining are, in order from here, Big Phil, Vicenzo, and Flavian. Big Phil cannot raise again, for he was the last player to raise, and a player cannot raise his own bet. Therefore, since all bets and raises have been called by the remaining players, the betting round is over.

THE SHOWDOWN

Following the conclusion of all betting in the final betting round, if two or more players remain, then the **showdown** occurs. It is the final act in a poker game where remaining players reveal their hands to determine the winner of the pot.

The player whose last bet or raise was called is the first to turn over his cards and reveal his hand. If his hand proves to be the best, he wins the pot and collects all the money in it. However, any player who claims a superior hand must show his. Players holding losing hands at the showdown may concede the pot without showing their cards.

The player with the best hand at the showdown wins all the money in the pot. In the event of a tie, or when there are two winners as may be the case in high-low, then the pot is split evenly among the winners.

If only one player remains after the final betting round, or at any point during the game, then there is no showdown, and the remaining player automatically wins the pot.

THE RAKE

The biggest difference between casino poker and private poker games is that in the casino games the house gets a cut of the action, called a **rake**, for their services.

The rake varies from casino to casino, and is usually proportionately higher in lower limit games.

Do not play in a game where the rake is greater than five percent of the total bet made. It is too much of an overhead. Find a more reasonable game where your winnings won't get dwindled to nothing by weighty house cuts. Always ask how much the house rake is before sitting down to play.

UNDERSTANDING THE RULES OF THE TABLE

Though poker is basically the same game played anywhere, at home or in the casino, rules can vary from game to game. Make sure that you're clear about the particulars of play before sitting down at a new poker game.

The most important questions to ask are:

1. What are the betting limits?
2. Is "check and raise" allowed?
3. Are antes or blinds used, and if so, how much?
4. What are the maximum number of raises allowed?

When playing a casino game, most of the above information is generally posted on a sign above the table, but if not ask the dealer or a player and find out. The additional question, "How much is the rake?" should be asked in casino games.

4. DRAW POKER
Jacks or Better • Anything Opens

JACKS OR BETTER

Also called **jackpots**, **draw poker - jacks or better** is a **closed poker** variation, where all cards are dealt face down (closed) and known only by the holder of that hand. It is played with two betting rounds. The first betting round occurs before the **draw**, with players having an opportunity to exchange up to three unwanted cards for new ones. (In some games, players are allowed to draw four cards if their remaining card is an ace, and in casino draw poker, players may exchange up to five unwanted cards for new ones.) The second round of betting occurs after the draw.

At the showdown, the highest hand wins the pot, or if all other players have folded, the last remaining player is the winner.

THE PLAY OF THE GAME

Both the casino and private versions of jacks or better require antes and these must be placed into the pot before the cards are dealt. Antes usually range from 10% of the maximum bet (normal size) to 20% (considered a high ante). In a $5-$10 game, a $1 or $2 ante would be the most common found.

Each player is dealt five face down cards. The deal begins with the player to the immediate left of the dealer receiving the first card and continues clockwise, one card at a time, until all players have received their five cards. The first round of betting begins at this point, with the first player to have received cards, the one on the dealer's left, making the first play.

To open betting in jacks or better, a player must have a hand with a minimum ranking of a pair of jacks. For example, a pair of queens, three deuces or a straight are hands that could open betting, while a pair of sevens or an ace-high hand could not. However, a player holding jacks or better does not have to open betting and may check his turn.

The first player to act must check if he cannot open betting (or holds jacks or better and elects not to). The next player, in turn, must also check if he doesn't hold the requisite opening cards. Players continue checking until an **opener**, the opening bet of jacks or better, is made.

Once an opening bet is placed, subsequent players, in order, may call, fold or raise the opener. Checking is no longer permitted. A bet has been made and players must call that bet to play for the pot. Play continues around the table in clockwise fashion until all bets and raises have been called.

If all players check on the opening round of play, the hand is said to be **passed out**. The cards will be collected and shuffled and the next player in turn will have the dealer's position. New antes will be required of all players and these are added to the antes already in the pot.

The draw occurs after the first betting round is completed. Each remaining player, beginning with the first active player to the dealer's left, can discard up to three cards (or five when allowed). The cards should be tossed face down toward the dealer who will issue an equivalent number of new cards from the unused portion of the deck. Players should draw in turn, waiting for the previous player to receive his new cards before making their own discards. The dealer draws last, if he is still in the pot.

Discards should be announced so that all players are aware of the number of cards drawn. Players who do not draw any cards are said to stand **pat**. This can be indicated verbally or by knocking on the table with the hand.

The second round of betting follows the draw and is begun by either the opener or the last raiser if there were any raises during the round. If no raises had occurred, and the opener has folded, the first active player to the dealer's left opens the betting. This player may check or bet as desired. Each succeeding player has the option of checking or betting, but once a bet is placed, active players must call that bet, if not raise; or go out.

The showdown, occurs after this betting round is completed. At this time, the player whose last bet or raise had been called (as opposed to players calling those bets) turns over his cards first. Any opponent who claims a superior hand must turn over his cards for verification. Players holding inferior hands may go out without revealing their cards.

The best hand wins the pot and gets to rake in the chips.

Let's return to our original crew and see how the betting works in a $5-$10 limit game of jacks or better. They're playing with a $2 ante, a high ante for this type of betting, and one which encourages aggressive early betting to "steal the antes." The pot holds $16 to start (eight players times $2).

These are the cards held after the deal:

Julian	K	10	7	3	2
Eddie-boy	8	8	10	4	2
Vicenzo	A	A	J	10	8
Fay	6	6	A	4	3
Donto	A	J	7	6	3
Flavian	K	10	9	8	7
Uncle J	J	J	5	4	2
Big Phil	5	5	5	8	7

Julian is on the dealer's immediate left and opens play.

Not having a hand of jacks or better, Julian checks, as does Eddie-boy, who holds only a pair of eights. Vicenzo can open and does so, flipping a $5 chip into the pot. Fay has nothing worth betting on and folds.

Donto is excited enough by his ace-high hand to call the bet, but it's a poor play. He's a big underdog with those cards and has little chances of winning.

Flavian's cigar is blowing smoke like a train coming down the tracks. With two players in the action and a large ante, the $25 in the pot gives him good pot odds to go for his straight (26-5, greater than the approximately 4-1 odds he needs to make the play justifiable) and he calls the $5 bet as well.

Uncle J. figures that the opener, Vicenzo, holds the jacks or better and probably at least kings or aces to have opened in such early position, and with two other players in the game, folds his pair of jacks knowing they're of little value. Big Phil tosses $10 into the pot, calling the $5 opener and bumping that bet $5 more. His three fives are strong cards, but if too many players are allowed to draw out against them, they could get beat.

Julian and Eddie-boy see that their free ride is over and fold in turn. Neither sees their cards being worth a $5 bet let alone a $5 raise on top. Vicenzo calls the raise and flips his $5 into the pot. Donto finally folds, poorer by his earlier $5 call. Flavian is playing for the draw and calls the $5 raise.

The raise has now been called by all active players and the first betting round is over. On this first round of betting, before the draw, all bets and raises are in the lower tier of the $5-$10 game, and are therefore in $5 increments. After the draw, all bets will be in the upper tier or in $10 increments.

Three players remain for the draw: Vicenzo, Flavian and Big Phil. Vicenzo throws his discards toward the dealer and draws three cards to his aces. Flavian calls for one card and after he receives his draw, Big Phil takes one card as well. Though Big Phil theoretically has better chances of improving his hand with a two card draw, his one card draw is a clever play, for opponents must figure him for two pair. Meanwhile, he's sitting pretty with his three fives, a favorite against his two opponents.

Here's how the hands look after the draw:

Vicenzo	A	A	9	9	2
Flavian	10	9	8	7	4
Big Phil	5	5	5	K	6

The opener, Vicenzo, acts first and bets $10. His aces over nines is a strong hand, and he figures it's a stronger hand than Big Phil's probable two pair. Flavian's train has slowed down and he folds. The four that he drew fell a little short of his needs and there's not much he can do with a 10-high hand.

Big Phil raises the bet to $20 (a $10 raise) and Vicenzo calls the bet. Since Vicenzo called Big Phil's raise, Big Phil must show his cards first and he turns over his trip fives. Vicenzo sees that he is beat, and mumbling something about his boss, throws his cards face down and concedes the pot.

Big Phil is the winner and collects all the chips in the pot, giving them a new home in his private stack. A new deal is ready to begin.

STRATEGY AT JACKS OR BETTER

As with all the other poker variations, the single most important strategy in jacks or better is to start out with cards which have good winning possibilities. The opening requirement of jacks or better tells us right off that any pair held which is less than the minimum opening hand of jacks is automatically a big underdog. For example, if a player opens the betting, what chances do a pair of eights have against this opener? We know that jacks or better are held.

Position is also an important consideration in jackpots. The relative position a player has in the order of betting affects the types of hands that should be played and how those hands should be bet. For example, if a player opens betting with a pair of jacks or queens in an early position, he's in a bad situation should his opener get raised by several players. You have to figure the raisers for at least kings or aces, possibly better, and with a lowly pair of jacks nobody is scared. The jacks are underdogs and must be folded.

Let's examine the minimum requirements for correct play in jacks or better.

Jacks or Better • Minimum Opening Cards	
First Four Positions (Early):	Kings or Better
Second Two Positions (Middle):	Queens or Better
Last Two Positions (Late):	Jacks or Better

In late position, with no openers yet made, the pair of jacks becomes a stronger hand. The jacks are in a good leveraged position, and an opening bet may be able to force other players out of the pot, effectively stealing the antes. If only one or two players call the opener, the jacks are in a decent enough position going into the draw to improve to a winner.

Once betting is opened, players holding jacks or queens should call only if two players or less are in the pot and no raises have been made. Otherwise, jacks and queens should be folded. Their winning chances rapidly diminish as the number of active players increase.

Four card straights and flushes have good potential and should be played to the draw, but only if the pot odds justify calling the bet. (See "How to Use Pot Odds.") However, do not raise with these hands, for at this stage they're speculative and hold no value. But should the draw fill these cards into a straight or flush, then you've got the goods to be raising and building up the pot.

Players holding kings, aces, and low three-of-a-kind hands should not only call the opener but raise as well. These are strong cards. If weaker and speculative hands are not forced out, these inferior hands may bury our favorites with a lucky draw. Against fewer opponents, there are less chances of this occurring. The more players that stay in for the draw, the higher the average winning hand will be, and the greater the opportunity that the kings, aces, and small trips will get beat out by an inferior hand that improves. Raise with these strong cards. Don't make the game cheap for dreamers.

On the other hand, with a high three-of-a-kind, such as trip 10s or higher, don't raise - call! We have a powerful hand which can win without improvement and want to keep as many players in as possible.

Do not play three card straights or flushes, or inside straights. An inside straight is a four card straight that has only one way of improving, such as 4 5 7 8. They are nothing hands, and the chances of improving are steeper than a canyon.

PLAYING A SMALL TWO PAIR

Smaller two pair hands, such as nines over threes, are deceptive hands in draw poker and must be played carefully. At first glance, two small pairs appear to be strong hands with good winning possibilities, but in reality, these cards spell trouble.

While a small two pair may stand tall before the draw, against three players trying to improve as well, they in fact become underdogs. If you're facing bets and raises before the draw and more bets after, your small two pair (with 11-1 odds against improving) starts looking even smaller.

Fold two small pairs in early position if the pot is opened ahead of you, or if you're in late position and three or more players are in the pot. In last position, against just one or two players, raise, and try to force them out.

THE DRAW

When drawing to a pair, the best odds of improving is to take a three card draw. Sometimes, however, holding a **kicker**, an extra card to a pair, can be a powerful bluffing tool. Players have to suspect your two card draw for three-of-a-king. Occasionally, use of the kicker in this fashion can really work to your advantage.

Drawing one card to a three-of-a-kind is a good bluffing strategy as well. Let's say you're playing a $5-$10 game. The first two players check and the third player opens betting with a $5 bet. The next player folds. You're in the next seat holding three eights and raise the opener $5. Players fold in turn around the table with only the opener calling the bet. He goes first and draws one card. You take one card as well.

After the draw, the opener bets $10, probably holding kings or aces up and figuring us for a lower two pair. We raise $10, banking on the 11-1 odds against him improving. He calls and then quietly folds his cards after we turn over our three eights.

Fold four flushes and four straights if they don't improve at the draw.

The dealer has a decisive advantage in draw poker, for he acts last. With marginal hands, he can come in the pot cheaply, or fold if the action is too stiff. He's in a great position to bluff, and being the last to draw can make use of his drawing strategy to a powerful edge. Due to the dealer's big positional advantage, draw poker is an excellent choice in dealer's choice games.

Play alertly and apply the winning strategies of poker to gain an advantage over your opposition and be a winner at draw poker.

Odds Against Improving Draw Poker Hands

Cards Held	Cards Drawn	Improved Hand	Approximate Odds Against
One Pair	3	Two Pair	5.3-1
		Three of a Kind	7.8-1
		Full House	97-1
		Four of a Kind	360-1
		Any Improvement	2.5-1
One Pair plus kicker	2	Two Pairs	4.8-1
		Three of a Kind	12-1
		Full House	120-1
		Four of a Kind	1080-1
		Any Improvement	2.8-1
Three of a kind	2	Full House	15.3-1
		Four of a Kind	22.5-1
		Any Improvement	8.7-1
Four Card Straight (Open Both Ways)	1	Straight	5-1
Inside Straight	1	Straight	10.8-1
Four Card Flush	1	Flush	4.2-1
Four Card Straight Flush (Open Ended)	1	Straight Flush	22.5-1
	1	Straight or Better	2-1
Four Card Straight Flush (Inside)	1	Straight Flush	46-1
		Straight or Better	3-1

DRAW POKER: ANYTHING OPENS

Draw poker: anything opens is played the same as jacks or better except that any hand regardless of strength may open the betting. Thus, for example, a pair of sevens could open betting in anything opens, or even a queen-high hand. Otherwise, the rules and methods of play are identical to jacks or better.

STRATEGY AT DRAW POKER: ANYTHING OPENS

The strategies in draw poker: anything opens are virtually the same as in jacks or better. Though any cards can open the betting, don't be fooled into opening or calling bets with anything less than you would do in jackpots. Whether the game requires jacks or better or requires nothing to open betting doesn't change the fact that you'll be dealt just as many good and bad hands in one game as in the other, and, therefore, the same minimum starting hands apply in strategy.

5. LOWBALL: DRAW POKER

This interesting variation presents a different twist on poker in that the lowest hand is the strongest in **lowball**, or **loball** as it is sometimes spelled, as opposed to the standard high poker game where the highest hand is the best. The ace is the best card in lowball, but, unlike high poker where the ace counts as the highest card held, in this game the ace is counted as the lowest card of a hand. The two is the next lowest card, and therefore the next best lowball card, and is followed in order by the three, four, five, and so on up to the king, which is the worst card in lowball.

In lowball, the high card counts in determining the value of a hand: the lower the high card, the better the hand. Hands are announced by the two highest cards held. For example, the hand 7 6 4 2 A is announced as a "7,6" or "7 high," and the hand 8 4 3 2 A is announced as an "8,4" or "8 high." Of the two above-mentioned hands, the "7,6" is the more powerful lowball total since its highest card, the seven, is lower than the eight, the high card of the "8,4" hand.

In instances where the highest values of two hands are equivalent, the next highest cards of the hands are matched up, and the lowest value of these matched cards determines the winner. Thus, the hand 8 6 4 3 2 is a stronger total than 8 7 3 2 A, and 9 6 5 2 A beats out the hand 9 6 5 4 A. When the competing hands are equivalent, such as 8 5 4 3 A versus 8 5 4 3 A, the hand is considered a tie and the pot is split.

The **wheel** or **bicycle**, 5 4 3 2 A, is the perfect lowball hand, and can never be beat. At best, it can only be tied by another wheel. 6 4 3 2 A is the next strongest lowball total, followed in order by 6 5 3 2 A, 6 5 4 2 A, and 6 5 4 3 A. And so on.

In lowball, straights and flushes are not relevant and do not count. The wheel, 5 4 3 2 A, is not considered a straight, but a perfect "5,4" while an 8 4 3 2 A, all of hearts is simply an "8,4" hand, not a flush as it would be considered in high poker.

Any five card hand containing a pair is a weak hand and can be beat by any five unmatched cards. For example, K Q 7 6 5 is a winner over 2 2 3 4 5. Two pair, three of a kind, full houses, and four of a kind are respectively worse holdings, and the odds of these hands winning are very slim indeed.

The term **smooth** in lowball refers to a relatively good back four cards, such as the hand 9 5 4 3 A, a *smooth* nine. **Rough** suggests a relatively weak back four cards, such as the hand 9 7 6 5 2, a *rough* nine.

Lowball is a draw poker variation, and, as such, is played similarly to high draw poker, featuring two betting rounds, one before the draw and one after.

THE PLAY OF THE GAME

Lowball is often played with an ante, and that bet should be placed into the pot before the cards are dealt. When no ante is required, a blind bettor is used, though sometimes both a blind bettor and an ante are part of the structure.

After the shuffle and cut, cards are dealt clockwise, one at a time, until all players have received five face down cards. The first player to receive the cards, the one at the immediate left of the button or dealer, is also the first player to act. For purposes of illustration, let's assume a $5-$10 lowball game using a blind. This first player, being the blind, is required to make a $5 blind bet and he promptly does so, flipping a $5 chip into the pot.

All bets before the draw in draw poker, high or low, are in the lower tier of the betting limit. In this example, all bets and raises are in $5 increments.

The next player to act sits at the blind's left, for play in all poker variations proceeds in a clockwise direction. He has three choices. He can call the $5 blind bet and remain an active player; he can raise that bet $5 more and place $10 into the pot; or he can fold his cards.

Play proceeds around the table until all players have made their decisions, either calling the blind and any raises that have been made, or folding and waiting for the next cycle of poker life to begin.

Now the draw occurs, and in the same order of the betting and dealing of the cards. The blind, if he is still in the pot, goes first, and can exchange up to five cards for new ones. Each active player, in turn, can exchange as many of his original cards as he likes, and should do so only after the preceding player has received his or her cards. Discards should be announced so that all players are aware of the number of cards drawn.

Players who elect to stand pat, not draw any cards, can indicate this verbally or by knocking on the table with their fist.

After the draw is completed, the second and last betting round occurs, and is begun by the blind, or, if he has folded, by the first active player closest to the dealer's left. All bets and raises in this round are in the upper tier of the $5-$10 limit, and are therefore in $10 increments. If the game was a $1-$3 games, all bets after the draw would be in $3 increments.

After the betting round is completed, we have the showdown, where the lowest hand collects the fruits of his or her labors, the pot, and all the money in it. If, at any point in the game, all opponents drop out of play, the remaining player would be the automatic winner, and he claims the pot.

The deal now moves to the left. In the case of a casino game, the former blind is now the button, and can enjoy all the advantages of playing the dealer's position.

STRATEGY AT LOWBALL: DRAW POKER

Lowball gives the knowledgeable player a tremendous advantage over uninitiated opponents, for the strategic thinking is different in this poker variation. Players are shooting for different types of hands, and it takes the high poker player a while to become accustomed to the peculiarities of the game.

The first rule in lowball is never to play a hand which needs more than one card drawn to improve to a winner. Unlike high poker, draws of two or even three cards are terrible draws and immediately single out a player as a weak opponent. A two card draw is a shot in the dark and is equivalent to trying to fill a three card straight in high poker.

To win at lowball, you must start out with cards that

can win. if the cards you're dealt are weak, throw them away unless you can get a free ride. For example, if you're the blind, and there are no raises following the forced bet, it costs nothing more to play and you should stay in for the draw. Always play further if there is no cost, no matter the cards. But if you're faced with a bet, fold, unless you've got the goods.

Position is important in lowball and must be considered in the opening strategies.

Here's our minimum opening cards in lowball:

Lowball: Draw Poker • Minimum Starting Cards

First Four Positions:
(Early)
8 high pat hand
7 high - one card draw

Second Two Positions:
(Middle)
9 high pat hand
8 high - one card draw

Third Two Positions:
(Late)
10 high pat hand
9 high - one card draw

Unless we hold an 8 high pat hand or have a four card seven high in early position, we can't call the blind's bet or make an opener ourselves, as the case may be, and must fold. We're too vulnerable to raises behind our position to call with these hands in the first four spots. There is a strong possibility that players will up the stakes in the middle and late positions. It is foolish to call hands in middle and early position if we will be forced to fold on a raise.

Do not call bets with anything less than the minimum openers in early and middle positions.

In late position, if a bet and a raise have preceded our play, call with a minimum holding of an 8 high pat hand or a four card 7 high draw.

With a 7 high pat hand, we hold a strong hand and should play aggressively. Raise the opener from any position at the table, or, if a raiser precedes you, re-raise.

When dealt a 6 high pat hand, you're in like Flint, and have almost a sure winner. Don't raise in early position, for you want to keep as many players as possible in the game. If, however, a player raises behind you, and it's just you and him plus maybe one other player, re-raise and build up the pot. There's something pleasurable about winning big pots.

6. SEVEN CARD STUD

High, Low (Razz), and High-Low

Seven card stud's three main variations - high, low (which is also called Razz), and high-low - all pack five exciting betting rounds into play. In each variation, players form their best five card combination out of the seven dealt to produce their final hand. In **seven card high stud**, the highest ranking hand remaining wins the pot. In **seven card low**, the lowest hand claims the gold. And in **high-low stud**, players vie for either the highest ranking or lowest ranking hands, with the best of each claiming half the pot; or players can go for the high-low pot and risk all to win all.

Players also can win the pot by being the last remaining player in the pot, either as a result of skillful bluffing or by attrition of opponents due to stiff betting.

In each variation, players receive seven cards. After the first three cards are dealt, two face down (closed) and one face up (open), the first betting round commences. The following three cards are dealt open, one at a time, with a betting round accompanying each card. The last card, the seventh, comes "down and dirty," and is the third closed card received by the players.

All remaining players now hold three hole cards and four open cards. These are the final cards they will hold.

One more round of betting follows the seventh card. Then the showdown occurs, where the best hand, or hands (as may be the case in high-low), claims the pot.

THE PLAY OF THE GAME

Following the shuffle and the cut, the cards are dealt in a clockwise direction beginning with the player to the dealer's left and continuing around the table, in order, until all players have received two closed cards and one open card. The two face down cards are called **hole cards**, as is the seventh card, also closed, that the player receives last.

All antes, if required, should be placed into the pot before the cards are dealt. Once an ante reaches the pot, it is like any other bet. It is the property of the pot and will belong to the eventual winner of the hand.

In the private high and high-low seven card stud games, it is the player with the highest ranking open card that starts the betting, or, if two or more players hold equivalent values, the high card player closest to the dealer's left begins play first. The high card player must bet to open play on **third street**, the name for this betting round, the first in seven card stud. It is a required wager. There is no checking on this round. Subsequent players must either call the bet, raise, or fold.

On all following rounds, the highest ranking open hand, in high and high-low seven card stud private games, opens the play. Also, from **fourth street** on (the name for the second betting round in seven card stud), the high hand may check to open betting. It is only on the first betting round that a mandatory opening bet is required.

In casino versions of seven card high stud, unlike

the private game, the player holding the lowest open card must open betting, or when two players have identically valued low cards, the player with the lower ranked suit plays first. For this purpose only, the suits are ranked in order of strength, beginning with spades, the highest, and followed in descending order by hearts, diamonds, and clubs.

For example, if the lowest cards showing are a three of clubs and a three of hearts, the three of clubs opens betting since it is the lower ranked three. Like the private game, in the first round of play, the player who goes first must make a required opening bet, and all following players, in turn, must call, raise, or fold.

In all subsequent rounds of casino seven card high stud, the player holding the highest ranking open hand acts first, and also like the private game, he may check to begin play.

In casino high-low seven card stud, the lowest card opens the betting in the first round of play, a mandatory bet, but thereafter, in all future rounds, the high hand acts first, and may begin play by checking or betting as desired.

In private seven card low stud games, the player holding the lowest open card (the ace counts as the lowest card in low poker) acts first and must make the mandatory opening bet. Conversely, in the casino games of seven card low stud, the highest ranking open card makes the required opening bet. There is no first round checking in these games either - players must call the opener, raise, or fold.

In all subsequent rounds, in the private and casino versions of seven card low stud, the lowest ranking open hand acts first and may check or bet as desired. For example, a player showing 8 6 2 A on board, an 8 6 hand, opens against a player showing a pair of sixes, 6 6 3 2, while a 6 4 2 A board would open against a 7 3 2 A.

Let's see how the betting works in seven card poker using a $5-$10 high stud game as an example. In the private game, the high card player must make a set bet, in this case $5. If the game was $1-$2, the opener would be $1, or in a $15-$30 games, $15 would be the opener. Subsequent players must either call that $5 bet, fold, or, if they want, raise that bet by $5 to make it $10 to the next player.

All bets and raises in this first betting round, called third street, are in $5 increments, the lower limit of the $5-$10 betting tier.

The casino $5-$10 game varies slightly in that the forced opening bet, the blind, is a $1 bet, and that the first raise is $3 only. (These numbers may vary depending upon the casino.) Thereafter, all bets and raises this round are in $5 increments. For example, if the opening $1 bet was raised $3 by the second player to act, the third player needs to call the $1 blind and the $3 raise, a total of $4 to stay in the pot. If the third player raises as well, the next player would need to call $9 worth of bets and raises to play.

When play returns to the opener in either the casino or private game, the opener must call all raises that succeeded his opener to stay in the game, as would any player who also had a raise follow his or her position. In the above example, the opener needs to call the $3 and $5 raises to play, while the second player, the first raiser, must call just the $5 raise.

The next round, fourth street, follows the conclusion of third street betting. Each active player receives a face up card and now holds a total of four cards, two open and two closed. Play in this round, as in all future rounds, is the same in both the casino and private versions, and begins with the player holding the highest ranking hand on board (or, in low poker, with the lowest ranking cards acting first), and continues around the table in clockwise fashion. When two or more players hold identically ranked cards, the player closest to the dealer's left will play first.

All bets and raises this round are in $5 increments unless an open pair shows on board, in which case players can open with a $10 bet. However, from fourth street on, the opening player is not forced to make a bet and may open betting by just checking. It is only on third street that a forced opening bet is required.

Once fourth street betting is concluded, another open card is dealt, giving players a total of three face up cards in addition to their two down cards. This round is called **fifth street**, and all bets and raises on this round and the following two rounds, sixth and seventh streets, are in $10 increments, the upper tier of the $5-$10 betting limit. (In a $1-$2 game, bets would be in $2 increments, and in a $15-$30 games, $30 increments.)

After fifth street betting closes, **sixth street** occurs with players receiving their fourth open card, giving all remaining players a total of six cards. Another round of betting follows.

Seventh street arrives, and each remaining player receives his last card face down. This is the final betting round in seven card stud and is followed by the showdown. Each player chooses five cards out of the seven total he holds to form his best hand. In seven card high stud, the best high hand wins, and in the lower stud version, the five best low cards will claim the pot.

Let's examine the showdown in seven card high-low stud to see how it differs from the high and low stud variations.

THE SHOWDOWN - SEVEN CARD HIGH -LOW STUD

Seven card high-low stud is played similarly to the high or low seven card stud games with the major difference being that players are actually playing for two halves of the pot: half the pot going to the player with the best high hand and the other half going to the player holding the strongest low hand. If a player holds the best high and low hand, he will take the entire pot.

High-low seven card stud is played as either declaration or cards speak. In **declaration**, which is predominantly played in private poker games, players declare at the showdown whether they're going for the high, the low, or the high-low end of the pot. Declaration is accomplished by each player hiding a colored chip in his fist and extending his closed fist over the table. At a given signal, players simultaneously open their hands and reveal their declarations: White chips are usually used for a low declaration, blue chips for high, and red chips for high-low, though using coins or different color assignments will work just as well for the declaration.

Of the players who declared "high," the best high hand wins that half of the pot, while the best low hand of players who declared "low" takes the other half. If just one player calls "high" and the rest "low," the player declaring high automatically wins half the pot and need not show his hand, while the low callers must compete for their respective half with the best low total winning.

And vice versa. If all players declare the same way, for example, all declare high, then the best high hand wins the entire pot. If all players declared low, then the best low hand claims the entire pot.

Players that declare "high-low" risk all, and must win both the best high hand *and* the best low hand or they forfeit the entire pot. It's an all or nothing proposition – they either win it all or lose it all. If a high-low declarer wins only one way, then he's out of the pot, and the best high hand and the best low hand split the monies.

Let's follow an illustrative showdown. Five players remain: Donto, Fay, Julian, Eddie-boy, and Big Phil. The first three declare "high," the fourth "low", and the fifth, Big Phil, goes all out and declares "high-low." (Flavian has already folded and both he and his cigar watch passively from the sidelines.)

Here's the hands they hold:

Donto (Declared high)	Jack high straight
Fay (Declared high)	Three Kings
Julian (Declared high)	Ace high flush
Eddie-boy (Declared low)	Seven-six hand
Big Phil (Declared high-low)	High: King high flush
	Low: Seven-five hand

Big Phil's seven-five hand is a stronger low than Eddie-boy's seven-six, but his king high flush is weaker than Julian's ace high flush, and therefore Big Phil, unable to win both ways, loses his high-low declaration and wins nothing. Julian and Eddie-boy hold the best high and low hands respectively, and split the pot. Had Big Phil declared "low" only, he would have won that half of the pot.

In **cards speak**, also called **high-low split**, the seven card high-low stud game played in the Nevada casinos, there is no declaration at the showdown. Players simply reveal their cards and the best high hand and the best low hand split the pot, or, if one player is fortunate enough to have the best high and low, he claims it all.

STRATEGY AT SEVEN CARD STUD: HIGH POKER

The first three cards received in seven card stud lay the groundwork for the future possibilities of a hand. Therefore, to build winners, we will only stay in with cards that have the right winning ingredients. Starting and staying with promising cards is especially important in seven card stud, for the five betting rounds of this game add up to a lot of bets and raises, and we want to give ourselves every chance of winning.

These are the minimum starting cards needed to enter the betting in seven card high stud:

Seven Card High Stud • Minimum Starting Cards
Three of a kind
Three card straight flush
Three card flush
Three card straight
Pair of 10s or higher
Low or middle pair with ace or king kicker
Concealed pair with face card kicker
Three high cards with two straight or flush

Starting cards of three-of-a-kind are powerful cards and are heavily favored to win. With these cards, you want to keep as many players in the pot as possible. Play low key on third and fourth street, calling bets but not raising, and later, on fifth street, if opponents start showing threatening signs of flushes or straights, bet heavy. You should either force them out or make them pay for the privilege of trying to buy their hands. However, if your trips turn into a full house, you have nothing to fear from straights or flushes and want them filling their straights and flushes. And how!

With three card flushes and straights, call third street betting, but do not raise. In general with poker strategies, it is only prudent to raise when either you've got the goods or when bluffing (and only under the right circumstances!). If our three card straight or flush doesn't improve by fourth street, it's time to say goodbye. Fold the hand. The odds against filling are getting too steep for the cost of calling bets and chasing cards for three more betting rounds.

Medium pairs that haven't improved by fourth street must be folded if either a higher pair shows on board or if raises precede our turn.

A key element in winning at seven card stud, or any poker game for that matter, is to lose as little as possible in the deals we don't win. Hand which have not panned out or have become underdogs must be folded. Avoid the temptation of playing "just one more card." That one more card costs money, and if it's not a sound call it's a bet out of our overall winnings.

To be a winner, we must wager with the odds, not against them. And those odds are defined by the cards held vis-a-vis our opponents, not based on the hopes of what might happen "if." Again, when a hand's possibilities fade and it becomes second best, bury it.

One indicator of how powerful hands may be going into the showdown is the intensity of the betting. If betting is heavy, with raises and re-raises, there is probably a reason – expect to see strong cards at the show down. If betting is light, with just a few players left, the average winning hand will probably be less powerful than otherwise.

It is important to play alertly and be aware of all cards that are dealt open in seven card stud. These cards give lots of information on the possibilities of improving a hand or on the chances of an opponent improving his hand or having certain cards in the hole. For example, if an opponent holds an open pair of kings and earlier you saw two kings folded, you know that no matter what kind of luck that player has, there's no way he can buy a third king. On the other hand, you'll be more hesitant playing for a flush if you realize that six of the clubs you need have already been played.

Heads up play is important in seven card stud and will make a big difference toward more profitable winning sessions.

STRATEGY FOR SEVEN CARD LOW STUD (RAZZ)

In seven card low stud, players use their best five cards out of the seven dealt to form the lowest hand possible, as opposed to high stud, where players look to form their highest totals. (See lowball: draw poker for ranking hands in low poker.) Strategic thinking in razz is different than high poker, for good lowball hands always start out as **drawing hands**, hands which need advantageous draws to develop into winners.

A player's first four cards may be A 2 3 4, a golden start, but if the following three cards received are a pair of jacks and a king, then that hands melts into nothing. On the other hands, seven card high stud presents situations where players are dealt lock hands for starters, such as the starting cards K K K. Regardless of future draws, these trip kings are heavily favored to win. Subsequent draws cannot diminish the inherent strength of those cards, while lowball hands which don't pan out die on the vine and become worthless.

However, to be competitive in seven card lowball, a player must enter the betting with strong starting cards, ones that can go all the way. Following are the minimum opening or calling hands that should be played in Razz.

Seven Card Low Stud • Minimum Starting Cards

Three card seven high or better (lower)
Three card eight high with two cards valued five or
    lower
Three card nine high, with the other cards being an ace,
    two or three
Ace plus five or lower card, and an odd card.

If none of the above combinations are held, the hand must be folded. You don't want to play underdog cards and contribute to other players' pots. If you can get a free ride into fourth street, take it, but hands less than the above-mentioned caliber cannot call a blind or opening bet. However, if you're the blind, and no raises occur behind your position, you're already in – take the free card on fourth street.

Relatively low supporting cards in low poker are called **smooth** hands, such as the trey and deuce in the starting hand of 7 3 2, or the four, three, two, and ace in the hand 8 4 3 2 A, a *smooth eight*. Hands where the supporting cards are relatively high are called **rough**, such as the six and four in the starting cards 7 6 4, called a *rough seven*, or the seven, five, four, and three in the hand 8 7 5 4 3, a *rough eight*. Smooth hands have greater possibilities than their rough counterparts and should be played more aggressively.

If an eight high hand or a smooth nine is made on fifth street, you're in a strong position and can play forcefully against players still holding drawing hands. You should raise their drawing hands. We're the favorite and want to either force them out of the pot or make them pay for every card they try to buy

Play aggressively against weak players for they'll stay in too long with inferior hands and when you've got the goods, why not make your winning pot that much larger?

STRATEGY FOR SEVEN CARD HIGH-LOW STUD

The splitting of the pot into two halves, one for the best high hand and one for the best low, makes seven card stud an action-packed and exciting game, and one where an astute player can win healthy sums against loose opponents.

And though there are more ways to win at high-low stud, players must not let the increased opportunities of winning pots tempt them into looser playing habits. The same winning principles apply - players must enter the betting only with good starting cards, ones which hold possibilities of winning either the high or low end of the pot.

Straddling the middle with hands that hold both high and low possibilities but are mediocre in both directions is costly and weak strategy. You can only work with the cards that you're dealt, and if the hand is not strong as either a high or low hand, then the hand is not strong, and the cards should be folded. We'll save our bets and play only with cards that can make us winners.

We'll enter the betting with the same starting cards we would play in either high seven card stud for the high pot or in Razz for the low pot. If our cards develop into potential two way winners, even better, but for now, we'll concentrate on winning at least one way.

Here are the minimum starting cards needed to play for the low pot:

Seven Card High-Low Stud • Minimum Low End Starting Cards

Three card 7 high or lower
Three card 8 high containing two cards 5 or less
Three card 9 high, with the two back up cards being an ace, two or three

---

Now let's look at our minimum starting high hands.

Seven Card High-Low Stud •
Minimum High End Starting Cards

Three of a kind
Three card straight flush
Three card flush
Three card straight
Pair of 10s or higher
Low middle pair with ace or king kicker
Concealed pair with face card kicker
Three high cards with two straight or flush

We can also play a concealed low pair, sevens or less, with a low open card, six or less, until fourth street. If the hand doesn't improve there, that hand should be folded.

Though we'll go in with a lot of hands, we'll also be quick to fold many of them if there is no immediate improvement on fourth street.

Three card flushes and straights should be ditched if the fourth card isn't bought unless fourth street position leaves us with a combination three flush or straight and three card seven high low. In that case, we'll take the hand to fifth street, and stay there only if we improve to a four card low or four card flush or straight. Otherwise, the hand should be folded.

Low or medium pairs that don't improve should be thrown away. With only half a pot to be taken, the odds don't justify playing these marginal cards. Similarly, the three high card hand, two straight, and two flush hands should be returned to their makers if they don't improve.

On the lowball side of the coin, a fourth low card must be bought to make the original three low cards worth playing. Three more betting rounds have to be faced, and with heavy betting and raising, trying to catch two more low cards is an expensive proposition, especially with only half a pot as the prize. However, if other low hand possibilities haven't improved either, and it seems our hand is still a competitor for the low pot, fifth street could be worth a play.

Low hands with flush or straight possibilities, such as the 7 5 2 of hearts or 5 4 3 of mixed suits are ideal high-low hands. They provide the double threat of taking the high and the low pot, and, if the cards pan out, of winning the high-low pot outright.

The nature of high-low stud calls for more aggressive play. When you have a lock on either the high or low end of the pot, bet forcefully. You want to create big pots and make the winnings that much sweeter.

7. HOLD 'EM

Hold'em, or **Texas hold'em** as the game is sometimes called, is steadily growing in popularity, and is perhaps best associated with freewheeling high action poker. Players receive two face down cards and combine these with the five face-up community cards shared by all the players to form their best five card hand. Altogether, hold'em has four betting rounds.

At the showdown, the highest ranking hand wins the pot, or, if heavy betting has forced out all opponents, the last remaining player is the winner.

THE PLAY OF THE GAME

The dealer deals cards one at a time, beginning with the player at the button or dealer's left, and proceeding clockwise, until all players have received two face down cards. The player to the left of the dealer goes first in this round and he is known as the **small blind**. The player to his left goes next, and he is known as the **big blind**.

Both these players must make a "blind" bet, mandatory opening wagers that create immediate action since they forces succeeding players to call these wagers to remain active. The small blind is normally smaller than the lower range bet in limit poker, while the big blind is typically equal to the lower range bet.

For example, in a $3-$6 limit game, the small blind might be a $1 bet, and the big blind, $3.

The required blinds can vary. Some hold'em games may even play without a blind, but in these instances players must either bet or fold. Blind or no blind, checking is not allowed on the first round of hold'em.

In casino games, a button is used to simulate the dealers position since a house employee actually deals the game. The button is moved clockwise around the table after each deal so that every player in turn gets to be the imaginary dealer and can benefit from that advantageous position.

Let's look at a $3-$6 limit game to see how the betting goes. The first player to act sits at the dealer's left and must open betting by placing a $1 blind into the pot. This is a forced wager that must be made regardless of how poor the player's cards might be. The player at the blind's left must either call this $1 blind, raise it $2, or fold. If this player folds, each succeeding player is faced with the same options: calling, raising, or folding.

If the blind gets raised $2, the next player must either call the $3 ($1 blind plus $2 raise), raise $3 to make the total bet $6 to the following player, or fold. After the $1 blind and initial $2 raise, all further raises during this round must be in $3 increments. The maximum number of raises permitted during a round is generally limited to three or five raises.

If no player has called the $1 blind bet, the blind wins the antes. The deal passes on clockwise to the next player for the next deal.

Once the initial betting round is over, three cards are turned face up in the center of the table. Known as the **flop**, these cards are used collectively by all the players. Each player now has five cards to form a hand – his two hole cards and three community cards.

The next round of betting begins, starting with the blind, or, if he has dropped, the player in the next active position to his left. Bets and raises during this round are in $3 increments only. In a $5-$10 game, bets and raises would be limited to $5 increments, and in a $15-$30 game, $15 increments.

On the following round, **fourth street**, a fourth community card is dealt face up on the table. Players now have a total of six cards possible to form their best five. Betting in this round and on the following round, fifth street, begins with the blind, or, if he has folded, the next active player to his left, and is in the upper limit. In the $3-$6 game, all bets and raises are in $6 increments.

In the $5-$10 game, bets and raises would be in $10 increments, and in a $15-$30 game, $30 increments.

There is no forced opening bet on fourth street (or fifth street, which follows), and the first player to act may check to open play. Subsequent players may check as well. If all players check, then the betting round is over and fifth street play will follow. However, should a player open betting on fourth street, all active players must call that bet to remain in the pot. On fourth street and fifth street, all bets are in the upper tier of the betting range. In a $3-$6 game, the opening bet and all future raises must be in $6 increments.

After fourth street betting, the fifth and final community card will be turned over in the center of the table. Players now combine their two hole cards with five of the community cards to form their best and final five card hand.

At **fifth street**, which this round is called, there is one final betting round, followed by the showdown. The highest ranking hand wins at the showdown, or, if all nents have folded, the last remaining player wins the pot by default, and collects all the antes, bets, and raises that had been made.

STRATEGY AT HOLD'EM

The first two cards in hold'em, the player's down cards, along with a player's position at the table, are the most important considerations in strategy. Like all poker variations, players must start out with solid cards to give themselves the best chances of winning.

We'll divide the starting hands into four different categories: strongest, strong, marginal, and weak.

STRONGEST STARTING HOLD 'EM HANDS

These hands are listed in descending order, best hand first:

AA
KK
AK (suited)
QQ
AQ (suited)
AK

The above six starting card combinations are the best in hold'em. They are strong enough to call from any position at the table and should be played aggressively. Excellent starting cards in hold'em, more than in any other poker variation, will hold up and finish as winners, so with these cards we'll be raising at the first opportunity.

We're the favorites in this game and want to build up the pot, but, at the same time, want to force out players

with strong or marginal hands. If the cost to ⌐
cheap, more players will take a shot at the flop.
players who stay in the pot, the greater the risks are tnat
a weaker hand will draw out and beat our favorite.

STRONG STARTING
HOLD 'EM HANDS

These hands are listed in descending order, best hand
first:

AQ
AJ (suited)
A10 (suited)
KQ (suited)

Hands holding an ace plus a high card are powerful
combinations in hold'em. If the flop, on fourth or fifth
street shows an ace, these paired aces tower over any
kings, queens, or lesser pairs that other players may hold.
It's tough to play picture pairs against an ace flop; you've
got to figure at least one opponent for a hidden ace.

Since only the best hand wins, lesser pairs must be
folded against an open ace.

Suited high cards give a player the twin chance of
forming a high pair or suiting up to a possible flush.

The hands in the strong category can be played in
any position, and though not as strong as the hands in
the "strongest" group, should still be played aggressively
for maximum value.

Let's now move on and see which hands fit into the
next lowest tier of rankings, the marginal hands.

MARGINAL STARTING HANDS IN HOLD 'EM

These hands are listed in descending order, best hand first:

JJ
AJ
KQ
A10
KJ (suited)
1010
QJ (suited)
K10 (suited)
KJ
Q10 (suited)
99

We'll play our marginal hands in hold'em as we would play marginal hands in the other poker variations – we'll stay in only if the cost is cheap. Our hands have possibilities, but are not worth the price of a stiff bet. The viability of entering the betting with marginal hands must take into account a player's position at the table.

The last position is the best for it permits a player to see what prior bets were made before committing his hand. Facing heavy bets and raises, marginal hands must be folded. However, if only a call is necessary we'll give these cards a chance at the flop. A good flop can turn these cards into favorites.

In early or middle position, players holding marginal hands can call the opening bet, but if there's been a raise the cards must be folded. If there is a raise after the initial bet has been called, this raise can be seen also, but we must fold in the face of a double raise, or in situations where yet another raise can follow.

WEAK HANDS

All other hands, ones not shown in the above three categories, should be folded. They are heavy underdogs with little chances of winning. If you're playing in a hold'em game requiring a blind or opening bet, by all means take the flop for free. But if it costs you to see the flop, fold immediately. It's much cheaper watching this round as a bystander.

8. OMAHA

A relatively new form of poker that has taken hold in cardrooms and casinos in the 90's is the very exciting Omaha games. Action is plentiful, especially in the high-low variations where multi-way pots and frequent raising make the game very exciting. More and more players are finding that Omaha is their game of choice.

Players will choose from a total pool of nine cards to form their best five card hand. Four of these cards will be in their own possession, dealt to them as down cards, while five cards will be face up in the community pool to be shared by all. However, players may not choose just any of the nine cards for their final five card hand, they must use two cards from their own set of four cards, and three from the community pool.

Thus, if a player were dealt four aces in the hole, only two of the aces would count toward the final hand. The remaining three cards must come from the board.

In the case of Omaha high-low, players can choose two different sets of cards to make their final hands, one set for the high hand, and one set for the low hand. For example, if a player held Q Q A 2, and the board showed Q K 5 7 6, two queens from his cards would be used to form the hand Q Q Q A K – three queens with ace and king kickers for high, and 7 6 5 2 A for low. The Ace and two, of course, would come from the player's own hand.

In all of these instances, as you see, two of the player's

down cards and three community cards were used to make the final poker hand.

THE PLAY OF THE GAME

In casino games, a button is used to simulate the dealers position, since a house employee actually deals the game. It is moved clockwise around the table after each deal so that every player in turn gets to play the dealer's position and can benefit from that advantage. Like hold'em, position is extremely important in the Omaha games with the player on the button being in the best spot.

Each player starts by getting four cards dealt face down, one at a time by the dealer, beginning with the player at the button or dealer's left, and proceeding clockwise, until all players have received their allotment. There is normally two blinds in the casino games, a small blind and a big blind, with the **small blind**, the player to the left of the button position going first, and the **big blind**, the player to his left going next.

Like all poker games, all action proceeds clockwise around the table, and the order of receiving cards and betting remain the same throughout the deal. The button will always act last, and the first active player to the button's left will always go first. Unlike seven card stud where the order of betting changes depending upon what cards are held on board, in Omaha, position remains constant throughout a deal. When a hand is completed, the button will move one place to the left, and for that deal the order of betting again would remain constant in the deal.

The big blind, the second bet, is normally equal to the lower range bet in limit Omaha, while the small blind is less than that amount. For example, in a $15-$30 limit game, the big blind would be $15. The amount of the blinds can vary from game to game.

After the blinds are made, each succeeding player must either call these blinds to stay active, raise the blinds, or fold. All bets in this round must be in the lower increment of the two tier structure: $15 in a $15-$30 game, $5 in $5-$10, $50 in $50-$100, and so on.

Once all betting has been completed, three cards are turned face up in the center of the table. This is the **flop**, to be shared by all players. There is another round of betting, starting with the small blind, or, if he has dropped, the big blind, or the player in the next active position to his left. (The blinds may have folded due to raises after their position.)

The first player to act may bet or check as he pleases—there is no forced blind bet in this round, or the future betting rounds. It is only the first betting round when the initial four cards are dealt that there is a blind. In fact, all players can check across the board if they so please, but of course, once a bet is made, succeeding players must call that bet (and raises if made), or they must fold their cards.

Like the first round of betting, all bets again are at the lower increment. In a $10-$20 game, bets and raises would be for $10, or for another example, they would be for $3 if the game was $3-$6.

When the betting is completed, a fourth community card is dealt face up on the table. This is **fourth street**. There is another round of betting and then **fifth street**, where the fifth and final community card is dealt face up in the middle of the table for all players to share. Betting on fourth and fifth street is in the upper limit of the two tier structure. In the $5-$10 game, bets and raises would be in $10 increments, and in a $15-$30 game, $30 increments.

Fifth street marks the last card the players will receive and the last betting round. It is now the showdown. Players now combine their best two hole cards with three of the five community cards to form their best and final five card hand. The highest ranking hand wins at the showdown, or, if all opponents have folded, the last remaining player wins the pot by default, and collects all the antes, bets, and raises that had been made.

OMAHA HIGH

In the high version, the highest ranking hand wins all the money at the showdown, or, if this player's best five cards are equal to an opponents, they will split the pot equally.

OMAHA HIGH-LOW 8 OR BETTER

In Omaha High-Low 8 or Better, there are often split pots at the showdown. In fact, there are often multiple split pots. For example, if two low hands are tied for best, and there is a high hand winner, the high hand will take half the pot, and the two low players will get *quartered*; each of them will split the low half, or get one quarter of the total pot. If there happened to be three low winners, they would split the low end three ways, or get one-sixth of the pot each, with the high side winner taking sold possession of the high half of the pot. Similarly, ties for high would be split the same way – all winners get an equal portion from the high half of the pot, or the whole pot if no player qualifies for low.

However, for there to be a winner on the low end,

that hand must be no worse than 8 or better. For example, a player would need to hold, say 8 7 5 3 A to qualify. A hand of 9 7 3 2 A would not qualify, even though it may be the lowest hand, and instead, the high end winner or winners would get all the spoils.

To qualify for the best five card hand, a player must use two cards from his four cards and three from the community cards. Thus, a player holding 2 3 4 6 with a community board of A 7 10 J K would not have a qualified low hand since only the 2 and 3 can be used from his own cards.

In casino games, **cards speak** determines the best hands at the showdown, while in private games, there is often a **declare**, with players announcing which part of the pot they're going for. Thus, if a player declares low in a private game and doesn't have the best low, that player wins nothing even if he happened to have the best high hand. Or if he declared both ways, high-low, and won only one of the ways, he would lose the entire pot. In the casino game, the cards themselves will determine the winners and losers.

STRATEGY CONSIDERATIONS AT OMAHA HIGH-LOW 8 OR BETTER

Omaha High-Low 8 or Better is a free-wheeling game that is marked by chips coming in from all directions. With both a high pot and low pot to go after, many players stay interested in the pot, especially since the river card on fifth street can so dramatically change a player's possibilities of winning.

The first four cards dealt in Omaha, the player's down cards, are the only cards he alone uses, and thus are very important in determining a player's chances of winning.

Like all poker variations, a player must start out with solid cards to give himself the best chances of winning.

There are great starting cards, good starting cards, and poor starting cards, like the other poker games, but what appears good or bad pre-flop, may change in a flash when the flop throws three more cards into the mix. And then there are two more community cards that will fall, opening up even more possibilities, and making and breaking other hands.

With such a volatile range of possibilities, hopes stay high for players, and betting can be fierce. Thus, one of the key strategies to follow in this version of Omaha is to play on the tight side and not get sucked into the rampant betting that sometimes occurs, not unless your possibilities are good enough. Speculation can lose you a bunch of money in a hurry in this game.

Other major consideration in Omaha High-Low 8 or Better is your position at the table. Since it stays constant throughout a round, and leverage is everything in Omaha, all plays must be made with position being foremost on your mind.

Starting hands with two very low cards give you a strong starting position in Omaha. An Ace and a 2 are good, for if three low cards fall on the flop, you have the nut low with two more betting rounds to go. Or if two low cards fall on the flop, say it is 3 7 J, you just need one more non-pairing low card for the nut low. Other starters such as 2 3, 3 4, A 3, A 4 are other good cards to have for they put you in good position to go for low.

Since low hands can be quartered, the best starters in Omaha 8 high-low would be ones that gave you both high and low possibilities. Consecutive suited low cards, such as A 2, 2 3, 3 4, give you excellent chances of going low and wheeling or flushing to a high hand. Combine these low cards with A A or A K, and these two way hands hold out many possibilities. The hand A K 2 3 with suited cards is very powerful with nut high and nut low straight possibilities. A 2 3 4 suited, gives nut low and wheel possibilities. High starting hands of A A K Q and A A K K can hold strong if the flop is all high cards, eliminating low hands from taking half the pot.

The relative value of high hands relates to the flop not only for the cards and possibilities it gives both you and your opponents, but for the chances it gives players to form low hands, which immediately devalue the pot by one half. This is a key concept that players going for the high end of the pot must consider in Omaha.

For example, for any player to qualify for a low total, there would have to be three low cards on board. If three low cards (8 or below) appear, it is likely that one player has a valid low. But if two low cards or less are on board, there will be no low hand, and the high hand will take the whole pot.

Thus, when making your decision on how to play a high hand, you must consider its strength on a different relative merit than straight high games if there will be a low hand grabbing half that pot. The pot is now worth *half* of what you might normally expect. This greatly affects the pot odds and how you need to view your high position.

When low cards will cut into your pot taking half of your action, you need a higher winning expectation and assurance of taking the high half to make the betting profitable. The great danger in high-low games that regular high or low players don't consider is this dilution of the pot, which makes betting and playing strategy considerations fundamentally different. That is why hands with the strength to go both ways are so valuable in high-low games.

9. THE 15 WINNING CONCEPTS OF POKER

INTRODUCTION

The knowledgeable player can consistently make money playing poker, but only if the game is approached from the proper perspective. As in any game of skill, there are important concepts that must be followed to be a winner. In this chapter, we'll discuss these concepts and show you how to recognize and implement the general winning concepts of poker to get an edge on your opponents and be a winner.

We've divided this chapter into fifteen winning concepts to isolate the factors that will improve your play and increase your winnings at the table.

You'll learn how to analyze situations and determine whether the relative strength of your hand is strong enough to call a bet or even raise, or whether, because of the bet size, the amount of money in the pot, your position at the table, or your knowledge of your opponents playing styles, you're better off folding the hand and conceding the pot.

A poker session is an accumulation of hands won and lost, and to come out an overall winner you must maximize your gains when you win and minimize losses when you lose so that the winnings overshadow the losses and ı have a profit to show. Of course, you never really know until the showdown whether you're holding the winning hand, but you can approximate your relative standing in the game and adjust play accordingly. Thus, when you're the favorite to win you'll get as much mileage out of the hand as you can.

Let's get down to the winning concepts of play now.

WINNING CONCEPT #1

Play Against Competition You Can Beat

As with everything else, being "good" at poker is relative. You may be a winning player at $5-$10, but if you moved your chips to a $50-$100 game, you might get eaten alive. Similarly, while you may be a good basketball player at your local park or chess player in your local club, if you start playing against the pros, you would be lucky to be even considered a scrub. And that level of player would be lucky to even dream of competing against pros who wouldn't even be good enough to be on the court with Michael Jordan or across the board from Garry Kasparov.

The point is, you can't win at poker unless you're playing against competition at or below your level. If you play over your head, well, you'll be over your head – it will be a one-sided affair, and you'll be on the losing end.

So rule number one, play with players you *can* beat. Don't be a patsy for players who are just too good for you. Don't play at a higher stakes game unless you're able to beat the level of game you currently play. And the converse of that statement holds true as well: If you're unable to beat the level of game you currently play at, don't move up a level thinking your "luck" will change. The only thing that will happen is that even better players will take your money at a faster clip. You're over your head. Move down instead. Get to a level where you can swim and you're the shark making money and not the fish being eaten.

For example, if you're at a $15-$30 game and constantly take a beating, you're not ready for the game yet. Why take the punishment? Get to the $5-$10 game where your skills may be more equal to the competition and improve your game there.

Take each level of poker game in stride. You can make more money at a higher stakes game, but only if you're good enough to beat that game. A busy cardroom may offer games for $1-3, $5-$10, $15-$30, $30-$60, $50-$100, $150-$300, or even higher. Just because higher stakes games are there, it doesn't mean you have to play them. Go slow, and work your way up as your skills improve.

WINNING CONCEPT #2

Fold When Beat!

Winning money in poker is not just about winning pots, in fact, being an overall winning player has probably more to do with losing less when your cards don't come in the running than it is about the pots you win when you've got the best hand! This concept is not appreciated enough by many players, who, despite winning enough pots, can't understand why they keep leaving the table with losses.

Folding when you're beaten at the table is one of the most important concepts in all of poker. More money is lost by players who consistently make bet after bet in clearly losing situations than possibly any other aspect of poker. Every extra bet contributed to an opponent's pot is one less bet out of your stack.

> *It's as important to make good folds in poker as it is to make good bets.*

To be a winner at poker, you must hold your money dear and value it like gold. There are good bets in poker, and there are bad bets, and if you can cut the number of your bad bets in half, right there, you will probably have turned the tide of turning losing sessions into winning sessions, and small winning sessions into larger winning sessions.

Never lose sight of this concept when playing. Do not play with cards that cannot win. This principle holds true at all points of the game in poker. When you lose, you should lose on hands you thought would be winners or which gave you good odds to play out as an underdog. Never lose on hands on which your odds of winning aren't worth the bets you're making, because you shouldn't even be playing them.

Folding when you're out of the running is precept number one if you are to be a winning player. Folding bad hands will make you more money in the long run than any other type of strategy you can pursue. This thinking should not be interpreted as advice to play like a rock, or to exit pots just because your hand is a dog, or to bet only when you're in the lead. Far from it. Smart poker play is balancing bets with chances of winning, and that includes playing for pots when you're strong, when you're trailing, and sometimes when you're weak.

When you do play second best or worse hands, it is because they give you good value – your long term expectation is to win money in this situation. You may be an underdog in a hand, but if overall, playing this type of hand gives you more profits than losses, it is correct to play them. Playing only good hands will mark you as predictable, and playing too many bad hands will bury you in losses. You must strike a balance in between for maximum results.

When do you know when a hand is a correct play? It is not always easy to figure out just what the right move is in a game, even on hindsight, but that's what makes poker so fascinating. However, experience and study will get you in the right direction.

Your goal in poker must be to win money. Having constant action and being part of every pot is a losing strategy, for by definition, it means you're playing in too many pots, with too many inferior hands, for too long. This is not a winning strategy. At the least, you need to start with cards that can win. Let's look at that concept now.

WINNING CONCEPT #3

Play with Starting Cards that Can Win

Sometimes you're dealt playable starting cards, sometimes you're not. Obviously, in the first case, you'll play the playable hands and see where they take you as the deal goes on. But in the second instance, where your cards are not promising and you're a big underdog, the proper strategy is to fold.

Too many players start out a hand with weak cards that have little hope of improvement, and yet will initiate bets, call other player's bets, and even put themselves in situations where they can be raised and have to cough up yet another bet – all this in situations where their hand doesn't warrant a single bet in the first place!

The object in poker is to have the best hand at the showdown, which means that to win you must enter into the betting with hands that have a reasonable chance of winning. You won't win every hand you enter, and if you did, there would rarely be any opponents contesting those pots. You must however, win enough money in the pots you do win to cover the losses from other pots you fall short in. To make this a mathematically sound pursuit, you need to bet, to some degree, in proportion to your winning chances. On a simplistic level, that means betting whenever you have a reasonable chance of winning, and folding when you don't.

The biggest mistake weak players make is playing too many hands. They're hypnotized by the action and don't want to miss any opportunities of catching a card that can make their hand a winner. Weak players will call bets and raises with inferior hands, incessantly waiting for a golden card that will take them down the yellow brick road. Now and again, underdog hands will draw out to win pots, but the wizard won't always be there and that type of play will ultimately result in heavy losses.

You have to avoid the temptation to play poor starting hands just for the sake of getting action. If you're playing to win, you must be selective in the cards you play.

WINNING CONCEPT #4

The Goal is to Win Money, Not Pots

There is a misconception among many players that winning more pots equates to being a bigger winner at the tables. In fact, the opposite is true! Weaker players tend to win more pots than stronger players because they're playing too many hands. Naturally, the more hands you play to the end, the more hands you will win, but that doesn't make for more profits. Every pot contested comes at a cost, and when many are contested and lost, it leads to a mighty bad day.

As the pros say, life is one long poker game. The goal is to win money, not pots. There is a significant difference between the two. After all, at the end of a poker session you're not going to measure your results by how many pots you won, and you probably won't even know the number. Neither will anyone else in the game. Nobody ever asks you how many pots you won, just simply, "Did you win?"

Wining is what counts in poker, the final result. And that should be your goal.

> *Life is one long poker game.*

WINNING CONCEPT #5

Understand the Importance of Playing Position

Your position at the poker table is an important determinant in strategy decisions, for you must always consider how many players will act after your calls, bets, or raises, and how they might respond to these plays.

Players acting **under the gun**, that is, first, are in the weakest position, for they not only have the least amount of information about how the opposing players are playing their hands, but are most vulnerable to raises and reraises. The result is that early position players must play a more conservative and cautious game. On the other hand, the player who acts last is in the best position for he gets a read of the entire table before acting on his hand, knows the action he is facing, and can adjust his strategy accordingly.

Players in the last position have leverage and flexibility, and can play a more aggressive game than early and middle position players. With the appropriate hands, last position players are in an excellent position to raise or bluff opponents out of the pot, and using this favorable position, they can steal more antes than any other spot at the table. If the action is light, they have the luxury of watching all the preceding action and coming in cheaply without fear of a reraise since their wagers will cap the betting for that round. And if a bet and raise precedes the turn and they are facing a double bet with a marginal hand, it is easy to fold without cost.

> ### *The deeper the player's position is, the more playable a marginal hand is.*

On the other hand, players holding marginal hands in early and middle positions have no such choice. Perhaps they feel their hand is worth a bet but certainly not two bets or more. The problem is that they cannot wait to see what happens. If a blind or bet precedes their position forcing them to call or fold, and several or more opponents follow their position, they are in a vulnerable spot with a marginal hand. This position is susceptible to any of the succeeding players raising that bet, and even reraising.

Well, if a marginal hand is worth but one bet, a player cannot take the chance of getting raised behind his position, and being whipsawed between several forces betting and raising each other. Thus, due to this vulnerable position, the correct play is to fold the marginal cards.

Marginal hands are only worth a play at a marginal cost. The deeper the player's position is, the more playable a marginal hand is.

As a general rule in borderline situations, go out with bad positioning and stay in with good positioning.

HELPFUL HINT

In dealer's choice games, the most advantageous games for the dealer to play are hold'em, Omaha, and draw poker because of the special positional advantages the dealer holds in these games.

WINNING CONCEPT #6

Be Aware of the Pot Odds

Pot odds is a concept that looks at the risks against the rewards of making a bet, the risks being the cost of a bet, and the rewards being the amount of money to be won from the pot. For example, if the pot holds $100 and the bet to be called is $20, then the pot odds are $100 to $20, or 5 to 1. You use pot odds to help determine if the cost of going for the pot is justified by the perceived chances of winning. Let's look at an illustrative situation to see how this works.

Let's say you're playing $10-$20 seven card stud and two opponents are left. You hold aces over threes and $40 is due our position. The first opponent, whom you figure for a probable three of a king, has opened on sixth street with a $20 bet, and was raised by the second player $20 more. The second player sits with four hearts and has straight possibilities as well, good scare cards against our two pair. With the $40 worth of bets, the pot now holds $240. According to the pot odds, should you call?

Of course, you don't know for sure what cards your opponents hold in the hole, but you figure your hand to be second best without improvement. An ace or three must be drawn to fill the two pair into a full house, the only way the hand can win. However, the hearts hand has one of your threes, and you noticed another three pass out of play earlier, leaving you, in fact, only two live cards, the remaining aces.

There has been a total of 28 cards revealed: the eight open cards of your opponents, your six cards and the 14 cards folded earlier by the other players. That leaves 24 unknown cards, and only two of those cards, the aces, can help your hand. The odds of improving to be a winner are 2 in 24 (1 in 12) or 11 to 1 against. The pot offers only 6 to 1, poor odds against an 11 to 1 chance of improvement. Aces up is normally a powerful hand, but in this situation the correct play is to fold.

The above hand worked well as an illustration, for only one card was yet to be played. Estimating pot odds value with more than one card to play becomes more difficult as more unknowns come into play. How fast will the pot grow? What future bets will have to be called? What new cards dealt will change our projected strength vis-a-vis our opponents? However, though more variables may come into play, and a pot odds analysis may become less exact, a rough cost of playing versus money-to-be-won calculation is always helpful in determining whether a hand is worth playing.

Let's look at a pot odds application for draw poker.

Pot odds dictates that four card straights and flushes should be folded before the draw if two other players or less are in the pot, unless the game is being played with a large ante. The chances of improving these four card totals to a straight or flush are approximately 4 to 1 against. With less than three players in contention, the money in the pot is generally not large enough to justify a call.

For example, in a $5-$10 poker game with eight participants and a $1 ante, the pot initially holds $8 worth of antes. If the opener is called by only one player, these two $5 bets boost the pot up to $17 in bets and antes. With only $17 to win and costing $5 to call, the pot offers less than the 4 to 1 odds needed to make the call a good play. The smart move here is to fold.

On the other hand, if the above game was played with

a high ante, say $2 per player, calling in the above situation would be an excellent play. The $10 in bets added to $16 in antes ($2 ante per player times eight players), fills the pot with $26 in bets and antes, 26 to 5 odds on the bet, better than the 4 to 1 odds needed to justify the call. Playing to the draw in this situation is an excellent move.

While evaluating pot odds is not always an exact science, since you're making some estimations and there are always unknowns, it is a useful and important evaluation tool that will help you make profitable strategic decisions in poker.

WINNING CONCEPT #7

Learn to Read Tells and Watch Out for Your Own

There is a whole science in poker devoted to the art of reading "**tells,**" the inadvertant tipping away of one's hand to opponents. Almost every player has their tells, some better hidden than others, and it is your job to not only seek out the tells from your opponents, but to protect against them finding yours.

There is a psychological and emotional reaction to every stimuli and event that occurs at a poker table, and a resultant physical expression of that reaction. The reaction can be expressed in some form of body language like a player shifting in his seat, leaning forward, or scratching his head, or in a small facial expression like a twitch or tightening of the eyes, or perhaps a faint grimace. The body is made of movement unless you're playing a carcass.

Learning to read tells is a master science, and if you

pay careful attention to the goings on at a poker table, you may occassionally be able to pick up signs that will clue you in to a player's hand or possible reaction to a situation. For example, some players lose interest every time they're about to fold, while others feign a loss of interest, and appear distracted when they hold monster hands.

A typical tell in beginning games is a player grabbing his or her chips when they're going to call a bet, even though the action is several players in front of them. Another is a player who more closely watches the action when he knows that he will be participating in the betting.

There are literally thousands of tells available for you to take advantage of – and guard against. For example, players may hold their cards differently or wear a different expression when they're going to fold. Other players can scarcely contain their excitement when dealt a big hand, and may express this in all sorts of obvious mannerisms – *obvious*, that is, if you're paying attention.

Look for vocal patterns and tones, the playing of chips, the holding of cards, facial expressions, where an opponent's eyes go (to their chip stack or an opponents, to the pot subconsciously counting the money they hope to win, to other player's eyes, or at least the one they fear most), the way a player sits, whether they speak more or less than normal, louder or softer, bet with more aggression (bluffing?) or more meekly, or toss chips so that they barely make it into the pot (disguising strength?).

Keep aware and watch what's going on. The patterns will emerge. Finding and using these tells is worth lots of money to the astute player. Having prior information on a player's intentions or an actual tipping off of an opponent's strength or weakness after a bet is made, is needless to say, a huge advantage in poker.

At the same time you search out tells in your opponents. You must protect against them finding yours. Learn to develop a "poker face," so that when you got the groceries, you can fill the bag.

WINNING CONCEPT #8

Disguise Your Betting Actions

Tells are not the only one way you can tip off your hand; being predictable in your betting patterns is just as bad. You must guard against being so consistent in your play, that not only do you know what you are going to do, but so do your opponents!

Poker is a game of deceit, where your actions, through betting, calling, and raising are a process in disguising your hand and creating doubts in your opponents minds as to the relative strength of your hand. One of the worst things you can do as a poker player is to become predictable. If your opponents always know that you bet, call, fold, and raise in the same situations, your play would be like an open book – they would feast upon you at the table.

If every time you bet or raise, more than your share of opponents drop out of the action, something may be amiss, and you must find that something to protect your pots. Whether it may be a tell, or a predictable betting pattern, you have to fix your playing so you get the proper value for your bets.

If you are pegged as a player who only plays with good hands, or one who raises every time a good hand is drawn, in no time at all, your opponents will pick up on this and adjust their play to take full advantage of the situation. For example, there are aggressive players who tip off good hands by suddenly playing meekly when their cards show strength. This unusual behavior often causes opponents to beware the quiet lion and drop out in marginal situations rather than meet the action.

To some degree, a good player *will* be predictable and that is okay. There is always a degree of consistency in good players. But at the same time, unless you want to play like a complete nut so no one will ever know what you're doing – except losing – there has to be a certain degree of unpredictability in your play. Part of being a good poker player is varying your play enough so that opponents never know exactly what's up your sleeve.

WINNING CONCEPT #9

Strategy for Playing Against a Loose Player

Loose players love action. They will play too many hands, call too many bets, and stay in games too long. By playing more hands, they will win more pots, but at the expense of giving away too many bets when they finish out of the money.

Loose players stay in pots with weaker hands, so you yourself can contest early pots against them with lesser hands than you normally would consider. In the late rounds, at the showdown, you'll call more often, for loose players will contest showdowns with weaker cards.

Bluffing should be avoided since it is difficult to bluff

a loose player out of the pot. Overall, a good strategy to pursue against loose players is to stick to a fundamentally solid game, playing a little looser than normal, and playing aggressively only when you have the strength.

WINNING CONCEPT #10

Strategy for Playing Against Players Who Bluff A Lot

Players who bluff often contribute a lot of money to pots and that is good, especially when you're sitting with a better hand than the bluffer. When you draw great hands, if the bluffer is in motion, you're in great shape and can play quietly while the pot is built up for you.

The general strategy against freqeunt bluffers is to call their bets more often when you have a hand that can challenge and beat the bluffer's hand if they don't have the goods. You have two ways to beat the bluffer. First, you can win because you already have a better hand. Second, your hand can improve enough to be a winner. Before calling, you must make sure your hand is strong enough on its own merits to make a stand, or at least has the potential to improve to be a winner if the opponent is not bluffing. Just because you know someone is bluffing, doesn't mean you need to play for the pot. Your hand must stand on its own.

WINNING CONCEPT #11

Strategy Against Tight Players

You should play a looser game against a tight player, a player who makes and calls bets only when he holds good hands. Since this player won't play with mediocre cards, you can force him out of the pot early with strong bets, at the same time saving money whenever your hand is mediocre and he bets.

You take advantage of his tight play by always figuring him for a good hand when he's in the pot. You respect his bets, for he's generally betting on solid situations. In borderline situations, you give him the benefit of the doubt and call his bets less often. When you do call his bets, you call with cards you figure can win, and if he raises, you make sure the pot odds and the strength of your hand justify a call.

WINNING CONCEPT #12

Strategy Against Players Who Don't Bluff

When in doubt, give the non-bluffer the benefit of the doubt and fold marginal hands. You save money against this type of player by calling less with questionable hands and by not having your good hands bluffed out by his scare cards.

This type of player is predictable, and that gives you a big edge in poker.

WINNING CONCEPT #13

Learning to Improve Your Play

Becoming a more proficient poker player requires that you pay attention to your opponents' moves and mannerisms during the course of a poker game. Hands and situations repeat themselves over and over again in poker, and it is the wise player who benefits from these experiences and can apply the knowledge gained to future hands.

While learning from mistakes is a great step in improving skills, a smart player also learns from his wins, and from other players wins and losses. He also learns from mistakes and the strong plays made by opponents. Every deal is a poker class that can provide a lesson, large or small.

It is the improving poker player that examines every situation and hand to see how it could have been played optimally. For example, on a lock-type hand, could an extra bet have been forced out of the losers, or could more players have been kept in the pot with a different betting pattern? Or on hands that lost, could they have been played more aggressively so that opponents could have been forced out earlier, or should the player have bowed out earlier himself, realizing that maybe the winner's betting suggested a better hand than could be beat?

A lot of poker knowledge is learned by observing. Watch your opponents and see how they react to the different situations that come up in a poker game. The more you learn about your opponents, the better your chances are of squeezing extra bets out of them, building bigger pots for yourself when the cards are right, and beating them more consistently.

How well you do in poker is not measured by the actual winning or losing of each hand, but by *how well you played that hand*. You must always examine your play and ask youself the question, "Did I play the cards optimally?"

Just because you won a hand doesn't mean you played it well, and conversely, just because a hand is lost, it doesn't mean you played it poorly. Perhaps you could have won a bigger pot, or perhaps you should have forced out another player and got lucky when he didn't draw out on you. Or in losing, maybe you stayed in one card too many, or shouldn't have played the hand at all.

If you constantly stay aware of how the game is being played, and keep track of the tendencies of other players, you can't help but become a better player. And playing better means winning more.

WINNING CONCEPT #14

Only the Best Hand Wins

Do not fall in love with your cards no matter how pretty they look. There are no prizes for second best at poker, only the winner takes the cake home. If you have kings over sixes on Fifth Street in seven card stud, and an opponent gets dealt an open pair of aces, the dirge has begun. If those aces are paired with a second pair, you're chasing with a dead hand. Aces up beat kings up in poker, and even though you may improve, those aces have an equal chance of improving. Unless you have very compelling pot odds, the romantic interlude is over – it's time to fold.

Sometimes strong hands must be folded in the face of heavy betting even though an opponent is suspected of bluffing. There is nothing wrong with being bluffed out of pots. That's part of the game. If you are never bluffed out of a pot, that means you're calling too often, and opponents are reaping showdown harvest with this loose play. Good players respect cards and can be bluffed. Weak players will never give up the ship until it sinks.

Don't worry about trying to scratch out a win in every pot. Just win the ones you can and minimize losses in the ones you can't.

WINNING CONCEPT #15

Be Smart With Money Management

There can never be enough said about how important money management is in the winning formula. From betting within one's means, to minimizing losses and maximizing gains, to emotional control, money management is the key to being a winner.

Be sure to read the money mangement chapter carefully and follow its advice.

10. PERCEPTIONS AND PLAYERS

In this chapter we will take a look at the human part of the game, the types of players you might face and the perceptions and counter-perceptions that influence the dynamics of a poker game. This is just a brief introduction to this aspect of poker, hopefully enough to get your mind flowing in the right direction.

THE GAME OF PERCEPTIONS

While many players evaluate the possibilities of what their opponents may hold judging by the cards they see and how they are betting, it is equally important to consider what cards your opponent thinks you hold. For example, while his play indicates types of hands he may have, so too does your play indicate some possibilities about what you may be holding. Poker, after all, is a game of logic and assessment, and intelligent players are always evaluating and reevaluating situations according to the actions of their opponents. While you are studying your opponents, they are studying you. What are you representing by your betting – a strong hand, a weak hand, a lock, are you bluffing?

As you analyze what you think they think you have, their actions become more understandable and you'll have more information to draw from in making your decisions. For example, in seven card stud, if your first three open cards are spades, and you've been betting according to a pattern that would lend credence to a flush, you'll have a lot more information about an opponent when their previous aggressive opening betting gets much more tentative as the third flush card was revealed.

RELATIVE GAME HAND STRATEGY

Poker is a game of relative strengths, where a lowly pair of sevens may take a pot in one hand, and a mighty full house may fall prey to a higher full house or even a four of a kind in another. It is unlike video poker machines where the schedule on the outside of the machines gives you an absolute payout for the poker hands you draw. In live table poker, what is one hand's rose, may be another's barren crop; it is all relative.

The beauty of poker is that while you never really know what opponents hold in the hole, you can make educated guesses based on the way they are betting from the particular position they sit. As we discussed earlier, position plays an important role in what hands a player can and cannot call, bet, or raise with. Evaluating the cards you see, the betting patterns of the table, the relative positions and actions of the players, and the dynamics of the hand, some reasonable deductions can be made.

Players who bet strong in early positions, for example, are advertising strength, because they'll need to weather possible raises after their position, while players that bet strongly in late position against little opposition, aren't necessarily playing the strength of their hand and may be playing the position.

And of course, while opponents come in a variety of

strengths and dispositions, they can be narrowed down to "types" and played accordingly. You'll soon learn which opponents play aggressively, and which won't budge with a bet unless they've got a strong hand, which ones stay too long in pots, and which players bluff too often or not at all. All this goes into the cauldron of your knowledge to be used with every bet in every situation to understand just how strong or weak your hand is at that particular moment.

Bets, calls, and raises are made for particular reasons, and over time, you'll get a better sense of what those reasons are. For example, if two opponents are betting into your four straight in seven card stud, and you believe they think you have a straight, you need to weigh that into your decision-making.

To be successful at poker, you need to know when you're standing strong, and when weak, when you're a virtual lock with the strength of your hand, and when your hand has possibilities but is trailing in strength to what you perceive your opponents are holding. Again, it's all a game of mutual perception.

Let's now take a look at the types of relative hands you might hold, and the general strategy to pursue playing these hands.

THE FOUR TYPES OF HANDS

You can define the types of hands you receive in poker into several categories, all of which, are relative to the situation you're facing. At the top of these categories are the "lock," a holding which is heavily favored to win the pot against all competition, and at the bottom rung, the weak hands, a holding which is rarely worth a bet. In between, are the strong hands and the trailing hands, the arena where most of your pots will be played.

In this section, we'll look at the four types of poker hands, and the general strategies you would pursue with them. We'll start with the worst poker hand, the "weak" hand, and work our way up to the strongest grouping, the "lock."

WEAK HANDS

This category describes hands with no better than longshot chances of improving to be a winner. These are the worst poker hands with long term losing expectations. The best strategy is to get out once there is a cost to playing the hands.

Weak Hand Strategy

Weak hands should be junked at the first opportunity. When you're a heavy underdog with little hopes of winning, you have no business investing your money in the pot and must fold your cards immediately. This advice applies to your starting cards, and it applies to your cards at any point in the game that they become weak. It doesn't matter how promising the career of your beloved cards may have started. Losing hands are losing hands. If you have trip kings and an opponent shows trip Aces on board, you're beaten baby. Your kings might as well be marshmallows in a rock fight, they're not going to do you any good.

Too many players chase pots with weak hands hoping for the lucky draw. That kind of strategy is costly and leads to consistent losing sessions. To be an overall winner at poker, you must avoid throwing away money on poor percentage plays. Every bet saved is that much richer your bankroll will be.

TRAILING HANDS

One step above the weak hand scenario is the trailing hand. You do not figure to currently have the best hand, nor are you favored to win if the hand is played out. Of course, a good draw will change that designation rapidly, but at the moment, you don't figure to have a strong enough hand to be considered a favorite or near-favorite; improvement is needed.

Trailing Hand Strategy

Relatively speaking, a trailing hand is an underdog, but does have some redeemeing value under the right circumstances. If the trailing hand can get into a pot cheaply or even grab a **free card** – the concept whereby a player can proceed to the next round for free because all players have checked – then this type of hand is worth playing to the next card. However, at the cost of a stiff bet, trailing hands must be folded and thrown to the wind. The winning possibilities of borderline hands aren't strong enough to warrant heavy investments into a pot.

For example, a pair of jacks, JJ, is a marginal starting hand at hold'em and holds some possibilities of becoming a strong hand with a favorable flop, but at the cost of weighty betting, or the threat of having to meet raises behind its position, this hand isn't worth a call. If an ace, king, or queen appears on the flop, the jacks begin to pale under the bright lights. A pair of jacks are heavy underdogs to the probable queens, kings, or aces of opponents, and will, in the long run, take heavy losses if they are played against a flop like this.

Position also plays an important role in the play of a trailing hand. From the last position, a trailing hand can be played because there is no possibilities of raises, while in early position, a call would be fraught with the danger of a possible raise after the position. This is not a situation you want with a trailing hand.

To sum up, trailing hands are worth a play when the price is right, but if the cost is at a premium, they're rarely worth betting on – save your sweet dreams for the late night, after the poker game. And save your money as well.

STRONG HANDS

This category represents cards which have excellent possibilities of improving into winners, and in fact are favorites or near-favorites, but can in no way be considered lock hands. For example, the starting cards A K in hold'em is a strong hand with excellent winning potential, but if all players stay in for the flop, the A K is subject to all sorts of flops making it an underdog.

Strong Hand Strategy

With strong hands you want to play aggressively. These types of hands have a good head start, but if you don't raise and force some players out, you take the risk of allowing mediocre hands to draw out and beat you. The more players in the pot, the higher the average winning hand will be and the higher the chance that a strong hand will turn into second best.

Let's illustrate this with an example. Suppose five players have a chance at winning, and given your starting cards, you have three of those chances. Each of the remaining players has one chance each. Together, of those seven winning chances, you hold only three of them making you an underdog to win the pot even though individually, you have the best chances of any one player.

But if you were able to force out two of those opponents, of the five total chances of winning, you would now have shifted the odds in your favor, having three of the five total chances.

This simple example is not that far from the truth. The more weak hands you allow in to see a card, the greater the chances are that one of those weaker hands will improve to be a better hand than yours. By playing weakly with a strong hand, you increase the competition, and decrease the chances of your strong hand finishing on top.

Your strategy with strong hands is to play aggressively right from the start and either force out the marginal and weak hands or to build up a pot which you're favored to win. With a strong but non-lock hand, you never should allow marginal or weak hands to play cheaply. If opponents want to see the show, they'll have to buy the tickets, at the price of your bets and raises.

If your previously strong hand appears to now be second best to a better hand, than you need to downgrade its relative value. *It is no longer strong.* The strong hand, by definition, means you're leading the pack. When that hand weakens to a trailing strength, the hand needs to be reevaluated according to the new situation.

It is important to adjust strategies according to the situation, for poker is not a game of rigid corrects and incorrects. You must be able to think on your feet, using your skills and instincts in the context of smart poker play.

To sum up: When you've got a good hand, you need to protect it by weeding out the competition so your hand has the best chance of taking the pot.

LOCK HANDS

Lock hands puts you in the driver's seat in poker. You figure to have a win and want to build up the pot as big as possible. There are two types of lock hands, the exposed ones in stud games where the strength of your hand is apparent or suggested to all opponents, and the hidden locks, where your fellow players have no idea of the strength of your hand.

For example, if you have three Kings in the hole in seven card stud, and King, eight, seven, six, as upcards, you're sitting with a monster hand that no opponent can see or perhaps even guess at. The strength is hidden. On the other hand, if three of those kings are on board there is strength exposed for all to see, and only an opponent who thinks they can beat your represented hand, or the possibility of a kings up full house or better would dare play for a nickel more.

Note that we're using the concept of the "lock" as the strongest relative position in poker, one that is a huge favorite to win except against the most uncanny luck by an opponent.

Lock Hand Strategy

Having a lock hand puts you in a powerful position where your only strategic concern is to get as much of your opponents money in the pot as possible. In one ideal situation, other players will have been dealt strong hands as well, though not as strong as yours of course, and will be bidding up the pot. In another ideal scenario, modest betting by many opponents will make the pot interesting and let players stay for more bets in hopes of improving.

Even though you would love to raise and reraise until your opponent's pockets are emptied, on a practical level, overzealous betting will drive your opponent's out of the pot, and that is exactly what you don't want to do. On the other hand, overly timid betting, if it's not your style for the situation, may very well clue your opponents in that you've got the goods and are sandbagging them.

So you must strike a balance, gauging the situation for the way to keep the most players interested and contributing to a pot that will be yours at the showdown.

UNDERSTANDING LEVELS OF PLAY

Of course there are many levels and degrees of skill and aggressiveness among players, but to a great degree, skill levels can be grouped into several general categories. We'll take a brief look at each.

BEGINNING/WEAK PLAYERS

Beginning and weak players often share one tendency in common: they play too many hands and stay in pots too long. Bet after bet is placed into pots they shouldn't be playing because they don't recognize that they are not getting enough value for their wagers. This type of behavior is seen over and over again among weaker players. In this category, you can find the **rock**, the tight player who will only play with good cards. The rock's play is so obvious that all opponents without a strong enough hand fold at the very first sign of his activity. But even more prevalent than the rock are the legions of loose gooses, the players who spread money around the pot like it's going out of style.

Weaker players are weaker players for many other reasons as well, but the prevailing feature is that they play too many hands too long. They'll win more pots than the average player but at such cost that anything less than really good luck will probably spell losses for their session.

AVERAGE PLAYERS

Average players will also make too many bets but not as many as the weak players, and they will play a more solid game. But they are average players for other reasons as well. Besides contributing too much money to other people's pots (where instead they should be watching from the sidelines), they don't maximize the wins from their good hands, and drop out of hands they should still be playing. They have some basic abilities in reading the table, but can't compete with better players who will eat them for lunch.

Average players play good hands too weakly and allow opponents to draw free cards, thus allowing too many hands to draw out on them. When their hand is relatively strong, they'll call when the action comes their way, allowing players behind their position to come in for just one bet, a situation that a strong player would raise in to thin the competition.

Among average players will still be the fair share of rocks and gooses, only with some more skills than their more novice counterparts.

STRONG PLAYERS

What separates the average players from the *strong players* will soon be apparent at a poker game. The characteristic quality of a strong player is aggressive betting. Unlike average players who will frequently call in answer to a bet, the type of bettor pros term **calling stations**, strong players will sooner raise than call, and you'll rarely get a free card out of them. Action will be fiercer, and you'll soon know the meaning of having to "pay to play." Strong players develop fear among their opponents at a table and leverage every bet to the maximum effectiveness. When the situation is right, they'll punish opponents who have the temerity to bet into their position.

Strong players know how to read and drive the action at the table. They're tough players and make opponents earn every dime that is won against them.

THE VERY BEST

The very best poker players obviously excel in every aspect of the game, they're super aggressive, and have no fear of any bet thrown their way. They also have the uncanny ability to read opponents based on the action and play of the table, and this allows them to play poker at a championship level.

11. BLUFFING

The bluff! The beauty, romance, and drama of poker lies in the bluff. It's an integral part of poker and an art that matures with experience. There are several advantages to bluffing. The first and most obvious advantage is that a player can "steal pots" from better hands and win money he otherwise would not have seen. There is nothing more beautiful than chasing out a better hand and taking the pot for your own.

> *Players who are known not to bluff will, on average, win smaller pots than players who are known to bluff.*

The second advantage to bluffing is that when you're caught, you have put doubt in your opponents minds. They will suspect you for possible garbage every time you contest the pot.

This powerful weapon makes your play more difficult to predict, and will win you bigger pots when you do have strong hands. Players with weaker hands will feel compelled to call your position more often thinking that their hands may be better. While they are keeping you "honest," your winning pot sizes get larger.

Predictable play is costly in poker, whether in the home game, casino game, or club game. Players who are known not to bluff will, on average, win smaller pots than players who are known to bluff. That is a fact. Opponents with mediocre hands will know that it is senseless to compete against the rock, because the rock only plays strong hands. On one hand, players are saving a bundle by folding with hands that likely won't come in first, on the other hand, the rock is not getting as much value on his good hands as he should.

To be successful at poker, bluffing must be an integral part of your game. You'll not only win pots where your hand is not the best one, you'll also win larger pots because opponents will contest your winning hands more often.

There's no exact formula for successfully bluffing at poker for each game is its own ball of wax, tied up in the unique dynamics of the game itself; the psychology of the setting, the venue where it's played, and the players comprising the game.

Let's go over some important bluffing concepts.

TEN POINTERS ON BLUFFING

1. BLUFFING IN LOW LIMIT GAMES

In many low limit games, players simply cannot be chased from a pot. For one, the action is cheap, and the thinking goes, "What's one or two more bets?" For another, low limit games attract players who can't be chased out of a pot with anything short of an elephant stampede. They will call bet after bet with terrible hands in losing situation hoping for the longshot draw that may (or may not!) give them the winner. They get those cards now and then, but in between, they get bled unmercifully.

If you're in a low limit game where players are not getting chased out of pots with maximum bets, there's no point in bluffing. If you can't bluff out an opponent, you need to redirect your strategy toward more basic play, working the cards a little more than the opponents.

Some players claim that you can't bluff players out of the pot in low limit games. That's certainly true for some games, but not for all. You'll find low limit casino games, say $1-$3, where players respect bets and can be bluffed. After all, to many, money is money, albeit the stakes are small, and they would sooner save their bets for situations with better prospects.

However, as each game has its own mix of players and particular temperament, you'll see what can and can't be done on a game by game basis.

2. BLUFFING IN MEDIUM-HIGH LIMIT GAMES

As opposed to a low stakes casino game, a bluff in medium to high limit games may register from the opening bell right down to the final round. With more money at stake, players are less subject to the 'friendly game syndrome' of staying in the pot a few rounds, and may immediately fold if the betting is too large for the value of their hand.

In casino and club poker games, a rule of thumb is that the higher the stakes, the better the level of player. As you play in higher stake games, your effectiveness in chasing opponents out of the pot will improve for the simple fact that good players respect situational betting and can be bluffed.

Of course, you have to pick your spots. Every game has its mix of strong and weak players and you'll need to learn as the game goes on who you can bluff, and who just won't understand they should be exiting the action. Poor players don't see the table well, and as we discussed earlier, don't realize that their hands can't support the action at the table.

Players who cannot be bluffed means players who play too many pots. If you find opponents like that in your game, that's good.

3. SMALL POT VS. LARGE POT BLUFFING

In limit poker, bluffing is more effective in smaller pots than large pots for the simple reason that, in large pots, there is simply too much money at stake for players to fold against the cost of a few more bets. With good pot odds and a lot of money at stake, it is hard to force savvy players from the sweet corn in the fields.

If an opponent is looking at a one in three chance of winning, and a bet to play would cost but one-fifteenth of the pot, it would be foolish not to play with such good odds.

Of course, bluffing opportunities may present themselves in any type of situation, but generally speaking, bluffs are much more effective in small pots for the reason given above.

With small pots, on the other hand, the thinking is opposite: opponents will feel it is not worth playing for a small pot at the cost for a big bet unless they either think they have you beat with what you may be representing, they have good pot odds, or they don't buy your representation of a strong hand. Otherwise, the pot odds simply aren't favorable to challenge for the pot with an inferior hand.

4. BLUFF THE RIGHT PLAYER

It's easier to bluff a good player than a weak one, and smarter to bluff a player who will likely bow out than one who won't. It's simply percentages. When targeting a bluff, choose situations that give you the best opportunity of success. It's common sense, but worth stating.

Many players seem to bluff indiscriminately, apparently uncaring about their target. That is a mistake. If you get a good scare card, say an Ace, don't try to power out an opponent who will likely call anyway. There is no sense trying to bluff a player who won't be bluffed, not unless you want to increase the pot on other merits.

Always choose your situations with potential success in mind.

5. AVOID MULTI-PLAYER BLUFFS

Bluffs are most effective against just one opponent. You may even be able to bluff two players, however, the more players in the pot, the greater the chances are that at least one player will call the bet.

With three or more players in the pot, there are too many possibilities for the bluff to fail. First, you are now needing to fool too many players, and second, perhaps one of those players you're trying to fool just has too strong a hand to go out with. Every time you add an additional opponent into the mix, the chances of that bluff working go down considerably, and your bluff, simply by the law of averages, is much less likely to work.

Thus, avoid bluffing when more than two players remain in the game.

6. TIME YOUR BLUFFS

Pick your spots carefully. Bluffing is a matter of timing and circumstance. When done judiciously, bluffing will make you a stronger player and a bigger winner. Bluffing too frequently can get expensive, for as opponents tend to believe you less and call you more, your inferior hands will be taking extra betting losses. That's not good for the bankroll.

7. BLUFF AGAINST SCARED PLAYERS

Watch for players who are losing heavily or have lost heavily and regained some of their losses. Psychologically, you have them in a position where they are more easily intimidated by your betting than normal. Players on a downward roll tend to play scared and are more easily bluffed when they don't have the goods. The more players worry over their winning or losses, the more leverage you have to push them around by aggressive betting.

Players who play timidly are also easily bluffed and bullied out of pots you can collect for yourself. They make for great targets.

8. BLUFF ON THE ROLL

When you're on a roll, and winners seem to follow winners, bluffing becomes a more effective weapon in your game. When you've got the fear factor going in a game it is a great time to ride that momentum with well-timed bluffs. Players are intimidated by the hot hand and respect bets more than they would otherwise.

9. OVERBLUFFING

It is one thing to bluff on occassion, it is another to constantly bluff. "Overbluffing" will drain you quickly as opponents quickly catch on to your ways. Bluffing is most effective in small doses. Overbluffing is another way to say "playing too loosely," otherwise known as "betting too much," and consequently losing too much.

10. FRIENDLY GAME SYNDROME

Many poker games, particularly home affairs and low-limit casino and club games, tend to be more friendly than competitive. Players stay in more pots and play deeper into the hands. In situations like this, where players want to see more cards before folding and the play is loose, it is difficult to bluff opponents out in the early part of the deal. Often, attempts at bluffing will be fruitless and it would be better to play a straight game.

However, further into the deal, the "sociable" players will begin to bow out as they realize that their longshots are no longer worth pursuing, especially when the larger bets start hitting the pot.

12. CLUB AND CASINO POKER

Playing poker in clubs or casinos is different than your regular Friday night game. The players and level of play tend to be more competitve, there is usually a stricter bet and rule structure, and while many players are there for fun, at the same time, there is a greater emphasis on winning.

In addition to tourists and local players, you'll often find local professionals grinding out a living at games of $5-$10 and higher. Players at these games are a lot less concerned in how your week went, as opposed to your buddies back home in the Friday night game, and a lot more interested in whatever green you're flashing that they hope to move into their own stack.

The play of low-level pros at $5-$10 may not be spectacular, but it will be steady, making the overall competition better than you may be used to. And as you move up the money tree, as we discussed earlier, you'll be running with bigger wolves. Playing against local pros at smaller stake games doesn't mean you can't win money. First of all, if you're a decent player yourself, you may be equal or better than the local pros. Secondly, there are always suckers at every game, patsies who never seem to learn a thing and are consistent losers contributing to everybody's pots.

I've emphasized lower stakes games above for a reason; the level of money being wagered in a poker game has everything to do with the level of competition you'll be playing against, and thus your chances of winning. The larger the stakes, the better the players. Pros playing in the $5-$10 game compete there because they're not good enough, gutsy enough, or well-financed enough to play at say, the $15-$30 game. The same applies for the $15-$30 and higher games as well. If the players could afford to profitably play for bigger stakes, they would move up to the bigger fish pond.

In casino and club poker, you're not playing against the casino, but against other players, and that's where the money wagered has everything to do with your chances of winning.

Let's look at this more closely.

CLUB AND CASINO POKER STRATEGY

A simple fact you must face in clubs and casinos, is that the higher the stake of the game, the higher the level of competition. The tourists and local players tend to be better (though there seems to be poor players at most levels of play), and most definitely, the pros are better.

Pros that squeeze out their living at $5-$10 will get picked clean at $15-$30, while $15-$30 players will get chewed up and spit out at $30-$60.

If a pro could earn money at a higher level game, he certainly would, for he's playing to make as much money as possible and there's more money to be had with bigger stakes. You can measure a pros' skills by the betting level of game he plays.

As a poker player, no matter your bankroll, you must

be aware of your skill level compared to the level of game being played. For example, if you're a fairly decent player, you may be able to compete with the tourists and local pros at the $5-$10 game, but at the $15-$30 game, the competition may eat you for breakfast.

Thus, your risk factor at higher stakes tables increases for far more than the obvious money management reasons – it increases because you're facing better players.

Poker in 50 States and Canada

Club poker can be found everywhere in the United States and Canada: either legally as in many states; openly tolerated, though not necessarily legal, as in some locales; or simply underground, as in every other place where open poker is not legislated into law.

As the 1990s move on into the milennium, legalized gambling is spreading like wildfire. States are finding that gambling tax revenues are a great source of income, especially in these hard times where governments are pressed for tax dollars.

And they figure, poker games are being played anyway. Why not legalize poker and get a piece of the action?

Deadwood South Dakota put themselves on the map and revitalized their entire area with the approval of gaming in their town. Bringing back the spirit of the Wild West, this old frontier town legalized poker as well as other casino games, and now boasts a booming economy.

Wild Bill Hickok's last poker game was played in Deadwood and the hand he held when he was shot dead at the table, Aces and Eights, is the most legendary poker hand of all. In poker parlance today, Aces and Eights, is known as "The Dead Man's Hand."

Dead Man's Hand

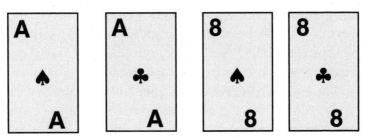

Legal poker is especially big in the West. Besides Nevada and California, the two biggest legal poker playing states, players can find legal poker clubs in Washington State, Oregon, Montana, North Dakota, South Dakota, and even British Columbia in Canada.

Many of these clubs offer discounts on buy-ins to help attract new players to the games. For example, on a minimum buy-in of $20, a club may give a new player $30 or even $40 in chips – quite a nice incentive. In return, the player must play a minimum amount of time or return the premium. If a player **busts-out**, loses his table stake, there is no penalty.

Poker clubs make their money either by charging each player a half-hourly or hourly fee for the seat, or as in Vegas, with a **rake**, a percentage of money taken out of the pot by the dealer as the house cut.

Poker clubs vary from the simple one game joints to opulent multi-game operations where the player will find fine dining, restaurants, a full-service bar, and even live music.

But poker is not limited just to the West. Indian casinos are springing up around the country and offering good poker games as well, and these venues, in addition to home games, plus legal, semi-legal, and illegal card rooms, give poker players ample opportunity to test their skills at poker pretty much wherever they live.

Wherever you decide to test your skills, keep your mind focused on winning, for that's what the game is all about.

Be a winner!

13. MONEY MANAGEMENT

To be a winner at poker, you must exercise sound money management principles and have emotional control. The temptation to ride a winning streak too hard in the hopes of a big killing or to bet wildly during a losing streak, trying for a quick comeback, are the most common factors that destroy gamblers. Inevitably, the big winning sessions dissipate into small wins or disastrous setbacks, while moderately bad losing sessions can turn into a nightmare.

In any gambling pursuit, where luck plays a role, fluctuations in one's fortunes are common. However, it is the ability of a player to successfully deal with these pendulous swings of the bankroll that is a vital element in the winning formula.

Luck certainly plays a role in what cards are drawn, and, in the short run, can sway its weight toward or against player. However, the overriding factor in poker is skill, and it is the play of those cards received that determines the end result.

Good players don't always win, just as poor players don't always lose. That's a fact of life at the poker tables. You can't win every hand or every session. However, if you stick by the winning principles outlined in this

book and follow the money management advice outlined in this section, you should end up a consistent
winner at poker.

The player that consistently gives his winnings back to
the table, is a player that doesn't give himself a chance to
win, in a sense, a player who *refuses* to win. No matter how
well a poker session is going, the player feels the need to
keep playing until the money is gone, and either subconsciously takes on some losing habits, or plays beyond the
timeframe where he or she has the winning edge.

This player I describe, is a loser, not a winner. He's a
gambler, not one playing with the percentages. This type of
bettor plays as if the goal is to lose. And if he can't lose it
today, there's always tomorrow.

For players hell-bent on losing, it doesn't take long for
the losing to catch up with them. We've all seen it happen
time and time again.

But losing is not what this book is about. It's about winning, and that's what I want us to concentrate on. What I'm
trying to teach you here is how to win. Part of this formula is
using the winning techniques and strategies we describe
throughout this book. Another part, the most important part,
is money management. If you don't handle your money in-
telligently and with a good plan from the start, you're going
to be a loser at gambling.

How you feel most definitely affects your overall chances
of winning, and there's no two ways about it.

A player that goes into a game with the goal of winning,
does everything he or she can do to achieve that goal. This
gambler will closely follow the money management advice
we lay down in this section. That's the mark of a winner.
They'll play within their means, they'll set reasonable limits, they'll control themselves at the table, and when they're

winning big, they'll make sure a good chunk of that money stays with them.

Smart money management necessitates that you have a bankroll large enough to withstand the normal fluctuations of a poker game and that you play for stakes within your financial and emotional means. You must be street smart, in a sense. There is no worse mistake than playing for money that is needed for rent, food, or whatever. The preoccupation to not lose that money will affect play and influence you to make decisions contrary to sound poker principles. This brings us to the most important gambling dictum.

> *Never gamble with money you*
> *cannot afford to lose,*
> *either financially or emotionally.*

This statement cannot be emphasized enough. Gambling with needed funds is a foolish gamble, for gambling involves chance, and the short term possibilities of taking a loss are real, no matter how easy the game may appear, no matter how stacked the odds. Crazy thing happen in gambling; that's what it's all about. But if you never play over your head, you'll never suffer.

Find a game whose stakes you feel comfortable playing, one where the betting range fits your temperament and emotional makeup. If the larger bets of the particular game you're playing make your heart pump too hard, you're over your head and need to find a game offering lower betting limits.

When you play with "scared money," you're easily bullied and pushed away from your optimum playing style. To win, you must go into the action with an edge and every asset you have, and not give your opponents a way to push you around because the stakes are too dear for you. They'll figure that out quick and you'll be at a heavy disadvantage.

Remember also that poker is a form of entertainment and, as such, must be kept in perspective. If the preoccupation of losing money creates undue anxiety, the entertainment value and probably your winning expectation will slip rapidly. It's time to take a breather. Recoup your confidence, and then hit the tables with fresh vigor. Play only with that winning feeling. Recognizing that emotions affect the quality of play is an important step in making poker an enjoyable and profitable experience.

BANKROLLING

As a rule of thumb, you'll need 15 times the maximum bet in a limit game for a sufficient table stake. For example, if you're playing a $5-$10 game, buy in for $150 (15 times $10). Similarly, in a $1-$3 limit game, you'll need $45 (15 times $3), and for a $10-$20 table, bring $300 (15 times $20).

What often separates the winners from the losers in that the winners, when ahead, leave the table a winner, and when losing, restrict their losses to affordable amounts. Smart players never allow themselves to get devastated in one session.

It is important to limit your single session table stake to the above mentioned limits. If you do not dig in for more money, you can never be a big loser.

As the saying goes, the first loss is the cheapest. You can't always win - catch some fresh air. Play again when you're fresh and brimming with confidence.

KNOWING WHEN TO QUIT

Part of the successful money management formula is knowing when to quit. You won't always be at the top of your game; you may be exhausted after hours of play, annoyed with another player, or simply frustrated by bad hands.

Whatever the case may be, the important thing to realize is that you're distracted, and that the loss of concentration will hurt your play. It's time to take a break.

You may even find yourself in a game where everything's going your way and you're winning in a big way, but getting tired. You feel you're a superior player, but have started making mistakes.

You hate to leave such a choice table. What to do?

Leave. Once you start making mistakes, you lose your edge, and may start handing back your winnings. Of course, it's tough to leave a game you feel is ripe for your skills, but when the edge is gone, it's gone. Take your winnings home with you.

MAXIMIZING WINS/MINIMIZING LOSSES

If you play poker regularly and your goal is win money on a consistent basis, you must not see every session as an end in itself and try to force wins where they just may not be there every day.

Again, you can't win every time, so the times you lose, restrict the losses to a reasonable amount.

You can't win every session, but if you're good, you

can win most. So just as important as it is to maximize your winnings at every session, by the same token, it's equally important to minimize your losses as well.

Five Money Management Principles

First and foremost is having a *winning attitude*. To be a winner, you have to *really want to be a winner*.

Second, you must *play within your means*. As we've discussed, you must play within your means.

Third, is the money part, *protecting your winning streaks*. Restricting losses is important, protecting your wins is equally important.

Fourth, you have to have *emotional control*. You must be able to control yourself at the tables, and not let yourself be overwhelmed by the gambling atmosphere and your emotions.

Fifth and finally, it's about *setting limits*. You can never allow yourself to take such a beating at poker that not only does your day or vacation get ruined, but you lose more money than you can afford to lose. And any time that happens, it's always a disaster.

14. THE GLOSSARY

Ace: The card with one spot. The highest ranking card in high poker; in lowball, the lowest and therefore most valuable card.

Action: Betting.

Active Player: Player still in competition for the pot.

Ante: Uniform bet placed into the pot by players before the cards are dealt.

Ante-up: A call for a player or players to put their antes into the pot.

Bet: A unit of money wagered and placed into the pot.

Bicycle: In lowball, the A 2 3 4 5 - the best possible hand. Also called the **Wheel**.

Blind: A mandatory bet that a player must make on the first round of betting regardless of how he or she feels about their cards. Also, the player making that bet.

Blind Bet: The blind bet itself. Also, a bet placed without looking at one's cards.

Bluff: The act of betting heavily on an inferior hand for the purpose of intimidating opposing players into folding their cards and making the bluffer a winner by default.

Bonus: Optional rule where a set amount is paid by all players to any holder of a high ranking hand such as a straight flush or a royal flush. Also called a **Royalty**.

Button: A marker used in casino games to indicate the dealer's position.

Buy-In: A player's investment of chips in a poker game or the actual amount of cash he or she uses to "buy" chips for play.

Call: To bet an amount equal to a previous bet on a current round of betting. Also known as **Calling a Bet** or **Seeing a Bet**.

Check: The act of "not betting" and passing the bet option to the next player while still remaining an active player. Players cannot check when a bet has been made. Also called **Pass**.

Check and Raise: A player's raising of a bet after already checking in that round. Usually not permitted in private games.

Cut: The amount of money taking out of the pot by the house as its fee for running the game. The cut is also called **House Cut**, **Vigorish**, and the **Rake**. The cut is also the act of separating the cards into two piles and restacking them in reverse order.

Dealer: The player or casino employee who shuffles the cards and deals them out to the players.

Dealer's Choice: A rule where the current dealer chooses the poker variation to be played.

Deuce: A card term for the two of any suit.

Down: A card dealt with its pips "face down" so that its value is known only to the holder of the card. Cards that are dealt face down are called **Downcards**, or **Closed Cards**.

Draw: The exchange of cards allowed after the first round of betting in draw poker variations.

Draw Out: The evolution of an inferior hand into a good one by the drawing of advantageous cards.

Draw Poker: Form of poker where all cards are dealt "closed," seen only by the holder of those cards.

Face: The side of a card exposing its value.

Face Down: When the side of a card identifying its value faces the table and is therefore hidden from public view. Only the holder of that card is aware of its value. Cards dealt face down to the players are also known as **Downcards** or **Closed Cards**.

Face Up: When the side of a card identifying its value is exposed and can be viewed by all players. Cards dealt face up are also called **Open Cards**.

Fifth Street: The fifth card received in seven card stud; the last round of betting in hold'em and Omaha.

Flop: In hold'em and Omaha, the first three cards simultaneously dealt face up for community use by all active players.

Flush: A hand containing five cards of the same suit.

Fold: The withdrawal of further play in a hand. Also referred to as **Going Out**.

Four Flush: A hand containing four cards of the same suit.

Four-of-a-kind: A hand containing four cards of identical value, such as K K K K, four kings.

Four Straight: A hand containing four cards in numerical sequence, such as 7 8 9 10.

Fourth Street: Fourth card dealt in seven card stud; the fourth community card exposed in hold'em.

Free Card: A betting round where all players checked, thereby allowing players to proceed to the next round of play without cost. Also called a **Free Ride**.

Full House: A hand consisting of three-of-a-kind and a pair, such a 7 7 7 K K.

Hand: The cards a player holds; the best five cards a player can present.

Head to Head: Poker played by two players only - one against the other.

High Poker: Poker variations where the high hand wins.

Hole Card: Card held by a player whose value is hidden from other players.

Joker: The "53rd" card in a deck bearing the drawing of a joker or clown, and sometimes used as a wild card.

Limit Poker: Poker in which the maximum bet size is set at fixed amounts. Limit poker is generally, though not necessarily, set up in a two-tiered structure, such as $5-$10.

Low Poker: A form of poker where the highest hand wins.

Misdeal: A deal deemed illegal and therefore invalid.

No Limit: Poker in which the maximum bet allowed is limited only by the amount of money the bettor has on the table.

Opener: The player making the first bet in a betting round or the bet itself.

Openers: In jacks or better, hands that can open the betting (consisting of a pair of jacks or higher ranking hands).

Pass: See **Check**.

Pat Hand: In draw poker, a hand to which no cards are drawn; also infers an excellent hand.

Picture Card: The jack, queen, or king.

Position: A player's relative position to the player acting first in a poker round.

Pot: The sum total of all antes and bets placed in the center of the table by players during a poker hand and collected by the winner or winners of that hand.

Pot Limit: A rule signifying that the amount of the largest bet can be no more than the current size of the pot.

Pot Odds: A concept which examines the cost of a bet against the money to be made by winning the pot and compares this to a player's chances of winning that pot.

Raise: A bet which equals a bet made previously in the round, plus an additional bet.

Rake: The amount of money taking out of the pot by the house as its fee for running the game.

Re-raise: A bet equaling a previous bet and raise, plus an additional bet.

Rough: In lowball, a backing hand that is relatively high, such as 8 7 5 4 3, a rough 8.

Round: The complete cycle of checks, bets, folds, and raises occurring after each new card or cards are dealt; the complete cycle of cards dealt previous to or subsequent to betting.

Royal Flush: An A K Q J 10 of the same suit. The highest ranking hand in poker.

Showdown: The final act of a poker game, where remaining players reveal their hands to determine the winner of the pot.

Seventh Street: The seventh and final card dealt in seven card stud.

Sixth Street: The sixth card dealt in seven card stud.

Smooth: In lowball, a backing hand that is relatively low, such as 8 4 3 2 A, a smooth 8.

Stand Pat: In draw poker, to draw no cards.

Straight: A sequence of five consecutive cards of mixed suits, such as 4 5 6 7 8.

Straight Flush: A sequence of five consecutive cards in the same suit, such as 8 9 10 J Q all of spades.

Stud Poker: Variation of poker where one or more cards are visible to the other players.

Suited: Cards of the same suit.

Table Stakes: A rule stating that a player's bet or call of a bet is limited to the amount of money he or she has on the table in front of them.

Tell: An inadvertent mannerism or reaction that reveals information about a player's hand.

Third Street: The first round of betting in seven card stud.

Trips: Three-of-a-kind.

Two-Way Hand: A hand that can be played for both high and low.

Under the Gun: The first player to act in a round of poker.

Up: A card dealt with its pips "face up" so that its value can be viewed by all players. Cards that are dealt face up are called **Upcard**s.

Wild Cards: Cards designated as "wild" can be given any value, even as a duplicate of a card already held, by the holder of that card.

DOYLE BRUNSON'S SUPER SYSTEM
A COURSE IN POKER POWER!
by World Champion Doyle Brunson

CONSIDERED BY PROS THE BEST POKER BOOK EVER WRITTEN
This is the **classic** book on every major no-limit game played today and is considered by the pros to be one of the **best books ever written** on poker! **Jam-packed** with **advanced strategies**, theories, tactics and money-making techniques - no serious poker player can afford to be without this **essential** book! Hardbound, and packed with 605 pages of hard-hitting information, this is truly a **must-buy** for aspiring pros. Includes 50 pages of the most precise poker statistics ever published!This is **three pounds** of professional poker advice!

CHAPTERS WRITTEN BY GAME'S SUPERSTARS
The best theorists and poker players in the world, Dave Sklansky, Mike Caro, Chip Reese, Bobby Baldwin and Doyle Brunson, a *book by champions for aspiring pros* - cover the **essential** strategies and **advanced play** in their respective specialties. Three world champions and two master theorists and players provide non-nonsense winning advice on making money at the tables.

LEARN WINNING STRATEGIES FOR THE MAJOR POKER GAMES
The important money games today are covered in depth by these **poker superstars**. You'll learn seven-card stud, draw poker, lowball, seven-card low stud (razz), high-low split (cards speak) and high-low declare; and the most popular game in the country today, hold'em (limit and no-limit). Each game is covered in detail with the **important winning concepts** and strategies clearly outlined and explained so that anyone can become a **bigger money** winner.

SERIOUS POKER PLAYERS MUST HAVE THIS BOOK
This is **mandatory reading** for aspiring poker pros, players planning to enter tournaments or those ready to play no-limit. Ideal for average players seeking to move to higher stakes games.
  To order, send $50 by check or money order to Cardoza Publishing

SAITEK'S GREAT HANDHELD CASINO GAMES!

The World Leader in Intelligent Electronic games

We're stocking these great handheld computer games again! These **exciting palm-sized** games fit into your pockets and can be taken anywhere - they're great travel items! **Easy-to-use**, you'll be playng in just a few seconds. Large LCD screens and superb sound effects bring the excitement and challenge of Las Vegas casino play to you. **High end** line has advance game functions, and streamline designs with lids. Includes automatic five minute powerdown.

PRO BLACKJACK - $39.95

Have fun and learn to win at the same time with this great blackjack computer. Has all the features: choose from 1- 6 deck games, and from 1-3 players at the table. Follows Las Vegas rules and allows $10 to $1,000 bets - hey big spender! Built-in hint key gives advice on all situations and even introduces you to card counting! Has superb casino sounds.

CRAPS PROFESSOR - $79.95

Brand New! The ultimate in craps simulations, this very handsome unit is an electronic trainer *and* game. Follows Las Vegas rules, make all the bets - pass, don't pass, come, don't come, free odds, buy, lay, place and proposition wagers! use electronic dice or roll your own (dice provided). Great casino sounds enhance experience. Comes with comprehensive book, hint cards, and winning strategy cards. Lots of fun!

PRO ROULETTE - $39.95

Beautiful unit has full layout and wheel with all the legal bets plus up to 12 wagers allowing from 1-199 bets! Make any number bet you want, game plays according to the real rules. Even better, up to three can play. Auto power off remembers game; turn on again another time and continue playing. Place your bets, and spin the wheel!!

Win at Blackjack Without Counting Cards!!!
Multiple Deck 1, 2, 3 Non-Counter - Breakthrough in Blackjack!!!

BEAT MULTIPLE DECK BLACKJACK WITHOUT COUNTING CARDS!
You heard right! Now, for the **first time ever**, win at multiple deck blackjack **without counting cards**! Until I developed the Cardoza Multiple Deck Non-Counter (The 1,2,3 Strategy), I thought it was impossible. Don't be intimidated anymore by four, six or eight deck games - for **you have the advantage**. It doesn't matter how many decks they use, for this easy-to-use and proven strategy keeps you **winning - with the odds**!

EXCITING STRATEGY - ANYONE CAN WIN! - We're **excited** about this strategy
for it allows anyone at all, against any number of decks, to have the **advantage** over any casino in the world in a multiple deck game. You don't count cards, you don't need a great memory, you don't need to be good at math - you only need to know the **winning secrets** of the 1,2,3 Multiple Deck Non-Counter and use but a **little effort** to be a **winner**.

SIMPLE BUT EFFECTIVE! - Now the answer is here. This strategy is so **simple**,
yet so **effective**, you will be amazed. With a **minimum of effort**, this remarkable strategy, which we also call the 1,2,3 (as easy as 1,2,3), allows you to win without studiously following cards. Drink, converse with your fellow players or dealer - they'll never suspect that you can **beat the casino**!

PERSONAL GUARANTEE - And you have my personal **guarantee of satisfaction**,
100% money back! This breakthrough strategy is my personal research and is guaranteed to give you the edge! If for any reason you're not satisfied, send back the materials unused within 30 days for a full refund.

BE A LEISURELY WINNER! - If you just want to play a **leisurely game** yet have the
expectation of winning, the answer is here. Not as powerful as a card counting strategy, but **powerful enough to make you a winner** - with the odds!!!

EXTRA BONUS! - Complete listing of all options and variations at blackjack and how
they affect the player. ($5.00 Value!)

EXTRA, EXTRA BONUS!! - Not really a bonus since we can't sell you the strategy
without protecting you against getting barred. The 1,000 word essay, *"How to Disguise the Fact That You're an Expert,"* and the 1,500 word *"How Not To Get Barred,"* are also included free. ($15.00 Value)

To Order, send ~~$75~~ $50 (plus postage and handling) by check or money order to:
Cardoza Publishing, P.O. Box 1500, Cooper Station, New York, NY 10276

$25 OFF! (Only $50 With This Coupon!)

Yes! I want to be a winner at blackjack! Please rush me the **Cardoza Multiple Deck Non-Counter** (The **1,2,3 Strategy**). I understand that all the two bonus essays, and the "Options and Variations" Charts all will be included **absolutely free**! Enclosed is a check or money order for $50 (plus postage and handling) made out to:
Cardoza Publishing, P.O. Box 1500, Cooper Station, New York, NY 10276

MC/Visa/Amex Orders Toll-Free in U.S. & Canada, 1-800-577-WINS

Include $5.00 postage/handling for U.S. orders; $10.00 for Canada/Mexico; HI/AK, other countries, $20.00. Outside U.S., money order payable in U.S. dollars on U.S. bank only.

NAME _____

ADDRESS _____

CITY _____ STATE _____ ZIP _____

MC/Visa/Amex Orders By Mail

MC/Visa/Amex # _____ Phone _____

Exp. Date _____ Signature _____

Order Now! 30 Day Money Back Guarantee!   CSB PO

158

AVERY CARDOZA'S CASINO

The Complete Casino Experience & Professional Gambling Tutor

For IBM-Compatibles (Windows 3.1/95 compatible)- Requires CD-ROM, 486/better, 8 MB RAM

65 GAME VARIETIES! - LOADED WITH FEATURES! - UP TO 3 CAN PLAY!

A GREAT TIME AWAITS! Enter Avery Cardoza's incredible **multi-player** 3D casino where **you're** *really* **part of the action!** 65 great game varieties include 1, 2, 4, *and* 6 deck blackjack, double odds craps, 40 different slot machines including progressive, 17 video poker machines, including progressive, big table roulette, and keno with a 100,000 game memory. **It's all here!**

YOU HAVE COMPLETE INTERACTION! Choose any of 4 ways to roll the dice *and* how long to roll 'em in craps; play up to three hands in blackjack; go for a royal flush in video poker; pull for the slots jackpot; make over 150 roulette bets; bet keno anytime - game is always playing!

INTERACTIVE 3D DEALERS ALSO! Dealers shuffle, deal, call the games, and react to your every move. 1803 responses tied to 257 criteria makes for dealers so intelligent and realistic, you never know what they'll say or do!

EXPERT ON-LINE TUTOR! Don't know what to do? Use ***Ask the Expert*** to learn the best play for *every* situation in *every* game!; or use the *Coach* to alert on bad plays, or turn off to go solo!

FREE BONUS BOOK - $15 VALUE! Learn the rules of play and how to use **professional strategies** with your $15 Avery Cardoza strategy book - included **free!**

MORE PROFESSIONAL FEATURES! 577 statistical fields keep track of *every* vital stat: your percentage of correct plays, most profitable sessions, the number of full houses or straights, number of blackjacks, hours of play, peak win levels, hot and cold trends, biggest craps shoot or slots jackpot, average win per bet - and 500 more fields! Also displays all fields as graphs!

INTERNET CASINO BETTING?
Yes - You Can Now Bet From Your Home!

The Era of the New Casino! - www.cardozacasino.com

Yes! It's happening now from internet casinos around the world. You can now can play all your favorite gambling games – blackjack, roulette, slots, keno, video poker, craps, and more – right from your home computer and go for the big winnings, just as if you were in the casino.

Real Play & Free Play

At some sites you can play for free, but if you want to gamble for real from your home or office, internet gambling–the new casinos – has become a reality. Are you dealt a square deal? Is casino gambling on the internet legal? We'll talk about these isues and more.

Find Out More!

Our web site will keep you up to date and informed with the latest developments on this exciting new technology. Check out our site anyway, there's no charge!

FREE GAMBLING INFORMATION
www.cardozapub.com

You'll also want to check out the new web site for Cardoza Publishing. Here, you'll find out the latest information on all our publications, receive the inside privy on the debut of our **free** online **gambling magazine**, and be kept up to date on internet gambling, the latest gambling strategies, the tip of the week, hotel specials in Las Vegas, and other gambling meccas. It's all coming soon right at our web site, **www.cardozapub.com.**

We'll see you there!